NO COLLEGE, NO PROBLEM

NO COLLEGE, NO PROBLEM

THE ROAD TO A SUCCESSFUL BUSINESS
STARTS WITH GRIT, NOT A DEGREE

PHILLIP LANIER

MDP
MISSION
DRIVEN PRESS

Published by Mission Driven Press, an imprint of Forefront Books, Nashville, Tennessee.
Distributed by Simon & Schuster.

Library of Congress Control Number: 2025913098

Print ISBN: 978-1-63763-469-1
E-book ISBN: 978-1-63763-470-7

Cover Design by Studio Gearbox
Interior Design by PerfecType, Nashville, TN

Printed in the United States of America
25 26 27 28 29 30 LAK 10 9 8 7 6 5 4 3 2 1

DEDICATION

For Tracy, Phil, Langdon, Bailey, and Sierra.
And also Mom and Gran!

Honestly, this is probably the page that required the most thought. What I kept coming back to is this: Who I am today is a reflection of everyone I've ever interacted with. From the incredible people in the low-income neighborhood where I grew up, to my amazing ex-wife, my extended family, and the entire community at the church that shaped my foundation, this book is dedicated to everyone who has played a part in building me.

Thank you all.

CONTENTS

CONTENTS

INTRODUCTION

My teachers in high school used to tell me, "You have to go to college unless you want to dig ditches for a living!"

Man, oh, man, were they right—but none of us could have predicted that literally "digging ditches" would result in my owning an $18 million, multistate construction company with more than one hundred employees! Those were some very profitable ditches! As it turns out, there was a lot of money (and hard-learned lessons) in those ditches.

I was a D student on average, with a flurry of Cs from time to time, and I had to attend summer school my senior year to graduate because I failed English class. There was a huge push in the 1980s and 1990s for everyone to go to college. The "college or else" threat was real, but looking back, I realize some of the most successful local people I know moved into the trades after high school instead of getting that esteemed, must-have four-year degree.

Due to that same rhetoric that shamed people for not attending college, the US is now short on skilled trades in every way. Let's put this into real terms.

In an interview with FOX Business, television host Mike Rowe mentioned that for every five tradespeople who retire, only two replace them, and this has been happening for about eighteen years. He said it's hard to find a major corporation today that relies in some way on skilled labor that isn't struggling to hire.[1]

According to an article from *The Hill*, the US is expected to be short 550,000 plumbers by 2027.[2] Wow! That's a shortage of 11,000 plumbers in each state. Think about that. We all need plumbers, and when we need one, it is usually an emergency!

The site EducationData.org states that the average cost of a degree from an in-state university is $108,584 over four years![3] That seems like a lot, but that is not even the true cost. You also have to factor in the four years of missed income you could have had if you'd been working all those years—plus the four years of contributions you could have been making to your 401(k) or other retirement plan.

Now let's factor in that the average student graduates with $37,853 of debt.[4] Considering that the average hourly pay for someone with a bachelor's degree is $28.21 per hour (as of 2025), that is hardly an enticing reason to go into debt for college.[5]

According to ZipRecruiter.com, the pay for a skilled trade job is around twenty-four dollars per hour in the US.[6] It is basically the same pay, but you don't have debt, and you don't have to miss four years of income. Plus, if you are self-employed, you can triple those numbers—easily!

· · · · ·

I've learned that life will give you what you are willing to settle for.

Settle for less, and you'll get exactly that—less. A job you hate, a paycheck that barely covers the bills, and a life that feels like it's happening *to* you instead of *because of* you. But if you refuse to settle, if you push for more, life will meet you at that level. It won't be easy, and it won't happen overnight, but doors will open for you when you refuse to accept anything less than what you were put on this planet to do!

If you are reading this book, it means you don't want to settle. It means you want something more for your business and your family. I'm here to tell you, you *can* have a successful business and a thriving family life.

In this book, I reflect on the humble beginnings of my journey as a business owner. When I started, it wasn't about grand ambitions; it was about survival. I began by performing small, labor-intensive tasks like cleaning cars and picking up trash, all while figuring out how to navigate a path that wasn't laid out for me.

I was always content in each job but then would feel the itch to make a move. That is how I worked at more than twenty companies before the age of twenty-nine. I went from cleaning cars and mowing lawns on the weekends to having more than one hundred employees with gross revenues of $18 million.

My teachers were right: Without a college degree, I did end up digging ditches. And doing so helped me develop the work ethic to turn those ditches into a thriving business. And my experiences—both failures and successes—have forged a passion for helping others grow, not just in business but also in life.

Perhaps you are wondering if college is right for you. Maybe you went to college but your degree doesn't fit you now. Maybe you've already skipped college and are worried about making a living, or you have children in high school who are weighing their options. Please hear me when I say I don't *hate* college education. It is absolutely the perfect choice for many people. But it's not the right choice for *everyone*, and it's time someone said that out loud.

There is a lot—and I mean *a lot*—of success to be found without a college degree. My guidance counselors told me I was making a huge mistake, but that "mistake" turned out to be the best, most life-changing decision of my life!

And it just might be yours too.

1

STARTING ON EMPTY

*How Struggles Prepared
Me for Success*

I sold my company and effectively retired at forty-seven years old.

You might read that and think I had a big head start in life—maybe wealthy parents and an Ivy League education. You might think I'm a tech genius or some viral app developer. You might think I lucked into some unique product or service that made me a millionaire overnight.

Nope.

The truth is, I didn't have any real advantages—at least not the ones you'd expect from a successful entrepreneur. Sure, some people are born on third base, but not me.

I was raised in Fort Mill, South Carolina, by a sixteen-year-old single mom. I only met my dad once.

He struggled his whole life and was overcome with addictions to alcohol and drugs. I was obviously a surprise—a shock, really—but despite her young age and what I'm sure was enormous fear and intimidation, my mother loved me and did whatever it took to survive the best way she knew how.

Growing up, I never thought of my mom as young. She was just my mom. It wasn't until I was around ten or eleven that I started noticing how different my life was from the lives of my friends at church. I didn't understand the concept of being poor, but I did notice that their kitchen cabinets were always stocked, and their fridges were always full—even with snacks! I loved going to friends' houses because there was always endless food and, best of all, color TVs that didn't need antennas.

To save money, my mom had truckloads of wood dumped in our backyard, and by middle school, one of my jobs was to split it with an ax or a sledgehammer and wedges. We had a woodstove in the center of our seven-hundred-square-foot house, and it was my responsibility to keep the fire going. That was cheaper than paying for heat. We had an air conditioner, but electricity was too expensive, except for one special tradition: On the Fourth of July, we'd turn it on for an hour and sit beside it, soaking in the cool air.

Our backyard also had a garden that provided vegetables for our meals. My mom did whatever it took to make things work. Looking back, I'm not sure if she ever thought much about our situation—whether we were struggling or just living. We didn't talk about it; we really didn't talk much at all. She was busy surviving, and I was busy just being a kid.

Near the end of my senior year in 1993, I moved out of my mom's house and into Porter's Motel (the creepiest, nastiest motel in Rock Hill, South Carolina) with my girlfriend. She and I both worked at the local Hardee's restaurant. So, again . . . I wasn't really starting off with a silver spoon in my mouth.

I failed English my senior year. For graduation, which I did not qualify for, the school offered to allow me to walk across the stage and receive what was basically a blank piece of paper. A fake diploma? Just for show? That would have been too embarrassing—so I skipped graduation.

I needed to go to summer school to graduate for real, but I had a problem: Neither I nor my girlfriend had a car to get me back and forth. However, on the first day of summer school, I ran into Hugh, a guy I barely knew, who was one year behind me and also in summer school. Hugh was an extremely popular guy and the MVP of the football team. He offered to pick me up from that motel and take me back and forth to summer school every day.

To this day, I have no idea why he did that for me. I did not have anything to give him to repay him, and

I am not sure he would have accepted it anyway. It was as if God placed him in my life at that time, just for this. Tragically, Hugh passed away a year later before graduating high school himself.

He was only on this earth for a short time, but man, he played a big part in changing my life. I will never forget him.

I finally graduated at the end of the summer of '93 after passing the English class. No graduation for me, though; I just stopped off at the school to get my diploma. A lot of people I knew from high school were going to college, but I didn't hang around people who were on the college track. I remember people taking the SATs and PSATs, but frankly, that whole process intimidated me. We never talked about it at home. The conversation never came up about college or testing, so I didn't understand anything about the process. I just assumed college was for other kids—the rich kids.

My girlfriend and I worked at Hardee's until we were able to save up seventy five dollars for a broken-down Volkswagen Rabbit. It had a busted axle, so we parked it until we could save up the money to fix it. We were able to scrape together another seventy-five dollars for an axle, which I somehow installed myself after asking my uncle and the guy at the local auto salvage yard for help—and then we were in business.

My family paid for six months of car insurance up front for my graduation, and then I was in the fast lane. Well, maybe not the *fast* lane, per se. We had to add one gallon of gas and three quarts of oil to that car just to get to work and back each day!

This was the beginning of my working career. I had made zero preparations, and I didn't understand anything about adult life or what it would bring.

I had more than twenty jobs between the ages of eighteen and twenty-six—one of which lasted only three hours! I worked as a cashier at Hardee's and a cook at Denny's. I worked as a helper for a stump grinding company. I worked at a moving company. I picked peaches for the farmers market. I installed gutters. I even spent a couple of months working as a roofer. And I was fired from at least two jobs.

It's funny—looking back, a lot of these jobs provided me with bits and pieces of knowledge and experiences that God would use to build me into who I am today.

· · · · ·

God knew the skills I would need later in life. I now believe that's the reason I had those twenty jobs. While my family thought I was just restless, I see now that each job was part of a bigger plan. I needed to learn various skills across different types of work, and every experience added another piece to the puzzle of who I was becoming.

Often, we don't recognize the bigger picture when we're in the midst of struggle. The road ahead is rarely

NO COLLEGE, NO PROBLEM

clear, but every challenge, every bit of strain, is laying the groundwork for your future. If you're feeling the weight of your journey right now, take heart—you're not lost. You're simply in the process of paving your road to success.

✎ **ACTION:** Write down two skills you learned through various jobs that have benefitted you in your current situation. Then, write two skills you still need to propel you forward from here.

_____

_____

_____

_____

_____

_____

The groundwork was being laid for a future I didn't yet know. After my relationship with my high school sweetheart fell apart, I met and married the love of my life, Tracy, in 1997. Then, in the summer of 2000, at the age of twenty-five, I struck career gold. I found a job at an engineering firm that paid $12.80 an hour—more than I'd ever made. Plus, I got a company truck *and* a clipboard!

This is when I proved my high school guidance counselor right—without a college degree, I really *was* going to dig ditches for a living. My job was to dig holes with a hand-operated auger and use an instrument to measure the bearing capacity of the soil to determine whether it was suitable and sturdy enough to build a house on. One of the major benefits of this job was that it required daily contact with the engineers. I'd never interacted with people on this level. Just being in proximity to them and hearing their decisions about situations began to change the way I thought and processed information.

All the lower-level jobs I had worked—restaurants, warehouses, and moving companies—put me in a cycle of earning a check and then spending all of it, without making any long-term growth.

At the time, I didn't yet understand the power of surrounding myself with the right people and putting myself in the right places to create opportunities for success. However, by landing a job where I was the least-educated and least-experienced person in the company, I unknowingly positioned myself for growth. Being surrounded by people who were ahead of me in knowledge and success changed everything.

Simply put, you become who you surround yourself with. You get to choose whether to be around low achievers or high achievers, and that choice will determine your trajectory. It will either lift you up or hold you back.

You become who you surround yourself with.

I decided to use that opportunity to improve my life.

🖉 **ACTION:** Who are the people you have chosen to surround yourself with? List them. Is it time for an upgrade? By being intentional about who you spend time with, you can place yourself in a whole new world of thought, even if it takes manual labor to do it.

_____

_____

_____

_____

_____

_____

2

NEW GIG, NEW BEGINNINGS
How New Connections Started It All

Little did I know that everything I learned at the engineering firm, along with the people I met there, would provide everything I needed to start my own company.

Over the next two and a half years, I met countless construction managers all over the city. I found that if I worked really fast to knock out the tasks for the engineering firm, I had time to stand around and talk to the customers, which enabled me to build good relationships with the clients.

I also learned what the construction managers wanted and needed. For instance, I learned that they worked long hours and never had time to get their trucks or cars washed. So my wife, Tracy, and I started washing and detailing the cars of the construction managers and subcontractors at night and on the weekends after getting off work at the engineering firm. Then the salespeople reached out wanting their cars washed. That led to the site manager telling me he could not find anyone to install anchor bolts (bolts that hold the walls down to the floor in homes), so we started installing those in the houses and townhomes. This paid really well. We would earn a week's pay in four hours!

One day, one of the construction managers asked if I would be willing to mow his vacant lots. Homebuilders would typically develop fifty to one hundred acres of land and install the streets and underground drainage systems. Then they would build house by house until the community was complete. Throughout the construction process, the vacant lots for sale needed mowing every couple of weeks to keep everything presentable. At completion, the community would consist of two hundred to four hundred homes.

The homebuilder supplied me with a thirty-inch-wide walk-behind mower. Each day, I would walk and mow a couple of acres. Man, that was a lot of walking. I could look across the field and see the concrete guys laughing as I walked behind this puny mower.

These guys were actually my friends, and they would later help me out quite a bit with repairs when machines that I would purchase for the business would break down. I had no idea how to repair the machines, but Billy, a concrete contractor, came to my rescue every time I called him, dropping whatever he was doing to help me.

As mowing jobs increased, we started renting a tractor with a bush hog attachment to work faster and keep up with demand. One day, I rolled the tractor into a ditch, and within an hour, Billy was there shaking his head, laughing, and pulling the tractor out. He then took out a sledgehammer and beat the twisted sheet metal back into place. Then he patted me on the back, gave a laugh, and said, "Later, Phil."

I would not have made it if it wasn't for him.

By that time, Tracy and I were both working full-time jobs and doing all this extra work in the evenings and weekends. It was taxing, but we were trying to save money "for a rainy day" and pay down the mortgage on our house. We did all this work—what you'd now call a *side hustle*—for two years.

Interestingly, I had no idea that a side hustle would be born almost immediately (and would go on to become my career) from the new job at the engineering firm. You can't always see what is coming! Contrary to the glamorous stories you see on social media, it's a bad idea to simply quit your job, take out a loan, and dive headfirst into starting a business without first test-driving it. Many bankruptcies begin this way.

Starting your business as a side hustle isn't just about bringing in extra income; it allows you to refine your process, discover what works, and avoid unnecessary risk. It gives you time to build, improve, and adjust your side hustle before you're fully dependent on it for your livelihood.

Starting your business as a side hustle isn't just about bringing in extra income; it allows you to refine your process, discover what works, and avoid unnecessary risk.

Yes, there is no way around it: It takes a lot of extra energy and sacrifice, but if this side hustle is what you're truly meant to do, it won't drain you; it will fuel you. The passion you have will give you the energy to push through those long days and nights.

✏ **ACTION:** Consider your current employment situation. Write down two or three possible side hustles you have access to that *don't compete with your employer.*

_____

_____

_____

_____

_____

NO COLLEGE. NO PROBLEM.

3

TRASH, TRIUMPH, AND THE FIRST $4,000

Going from Side Hustle to Full Hustle

I n 2003, my hours at the engineering firm dropped from more than sixty-five hours a week to about ten to fifteen hours per week. And let me tell you, when you are living from paycheck to paycheck, having your check cut by 75 percent is devastating!

After working for a couple of weeks at the reduced hours, it was clear that we would not be able to pay our mortgage and bills like this, so I started making calls, trying to find more income. I remember it like it was yesterday.

I made a call to John Watson, a site manager at Ryland Homes, whom I met through one of the home-builders. His job was to oversee the entire jobsite. There were roughly one hundred acres of land with only the streets paved and vacant house lots freshly graded and waiting for someone to build a house on them. This community had already started because they had begun construction on fifty houses at the same time, so the jobsite was a mess from all the activity.

John said, "Phillip, go get some insurance, and I will let you pick up trash on my jobsite. You have to have insurance though. I can't let you work unless you are insured!"

I had no money, no resources, and no contacts. I didn't even know how to begin figuring anything out. John helped me by calling the main office at his company. They said I could buy "in-house insurance" through them, and they would just deduct 12 percent of my check. Done!

The next day, I went in to quit my job at the engineering firm . . . but no one cared. It only helped everyone else, because my ten hours per week could be divided among the other fifty employees.

I was now in business for myself, but the funny thing was, I didn't see this as a business. I could not see that far ahead or think that big. I just saw it as a job that had endless amounts of work. I was terrified and excited all at the same time! I had just turned twenty-nine a few months earlier, and I finally had something I could run with.

At the time, Tracy worked for an insurance company answering phones for ten dollars an hour. We asked Judy, an accountant who occupied a small back room of their insurance office, if she would help us do the paperwork to start the business. She agreed, but I can only wonder what she must have thought with both of us wanting to start a business with almost nothing.

She set up an S corporation for us—I had no idea what that meant—and then she asked a question that left me speechless.

"What do you want the name of your company to be?"

Holy cow! I had no idea. I had not even thought of that. I drew a blank and could not answer her.

A couple of months earlier, my grandparents had invited us over for dinner. My grandfather asked me if I was learning to use computers yet, which we definitely were not. Our grocery budget at the time was twenty-five dollars a week. There was no room for computers in that budget.

My grandfather said, "At least let me set up an email address for you."

I am probably the only man in history whose grandfather taught him about technology. I was way behind the curve! It was 2003, and I had no idea what an email address was or what to do with one. He proceeded to set up an email address: pandtl@aol.com.

I remember saying, "What is *PandTL*?"

My grandfather said, "Phillip and Tracy Lanier. That should cover you both."

To this day, I have no idea what prompted him to invite us over and do that.

And so, when Judy asked me what I wanted to name our company, for some reason, I thought of our new email address. At that moment, we decided to name the company PandTL Inc. She said it would cost $500 for the incorporation, and I used my credit card. Now that I think about it, I don't think she ever charged me for any of her time setting up the company . . .

When I showed up to John's jobsite the next day, it was less glorious than I thought. He pointed to a house being framed, then pointed to all the trash and shingle wrappers and soda cans in the yard, then proceeded to point to the big blue dumpster and said, "It goes in there."

It took more than a week to clean up around each of the houses, and Tracy came out to help me in the evenings and weekends. We realized we could not keep up, so we reached out to her family members and neighbors, and they came out to help us. We even hired a man who called himself "Bat-Mite." No one knew why this was his name, but we were desperate for help. If Bat-Mite was ready and willing, he was welcome. Our hiring practices were definitely in the early stages of development!

Looking back, I cannot even imagine what we must have looked like. What I am sure of is that it had to look hilarious. It was a buffet for me. I had never seen so much work in my life. The fellow subcontractors even helped us stay in business, in a way. They would look at us and not even bother carrying their debris to the dumpster. Instead, they would just throw it on the ground in front of us and smile.

Money was beginning to run very low. My anxiety was beginning to rise.

I checked the mail each evening. Bills, ads, junk. Money? Nope. And each day, I would take that mail and shuffle back to the house with the contents. Then, after five weeks of working, there was an envelope from Ryland Homes. I tore it open and there it was— my first-ever commercial paycheck for $4,000! I had never seen that much money before.

We had been out of money for weeks, just filling the gas tanks and buying crackers with credit cards. I must have set a speed record that day running back to our eight-hundred-square-foot brick ranch to show Tracy. But we didn't race to the bank to cash it; we just sat there and looked at it.

Tracy soon lost interest in the check and went back to what she was doing, but I folded the check, opened it, turned it over. I looked at it again. I just could not believe there was this much money out there.

That week, we paid off the credit cards, and for the first time in our marriage, we bought fuel and lunch with our very own money, not on credit. It didn't feel real. After that initial waiting period for the first check, they started coming in weekly. Some of the checks were much bigger, some smaller. But they rolled in. We didn't count them; we didn't have time. We just put them in the bank, got our crackers and sandwiches, and went back to work.

I watched many friends spend money they didn't have—buying new trucks and luxuries in anticipation of a big check. The expectation of future income often leads many people to overspend. Then, when the money finally arrives, it's already spent. I've seen this mistake cause countless problems.

Tracy and I, on the other hand, literally lived on crackers and sandwiches, doing whatever we could for fun without spending money. We didn't rely on what might come—we lived only on what we had.

• • • • •

The lesson? Live on the money you *actually* have, not on the money you *might* have later. Financial discipline now will save you from financial stress later on—and ensure that when the big checks do come, you can use them to grow, instead of just covering what you've already spent.

The lesson? Live on the money you actually *have, not on the money you* might *have later.*

✎ **ACTION:** Discipline yourself to say no to buying that new "thing" just because you're excited about a new business or a big payday. Instead, write down two or three ways to buy the most *inexpensive* items/tools to get the job done. It's neither wise nor fun to have awesome things but a puny bank account.

_____

_____

_____

_____

_____

_____

4

SEIZING THE MOMENT
How Saying Yes Changed Everything

One day, after some time had passed, John came to me with some news: He was quitting his job and going to work for another company.

I was terrified. In my mind, I had just lost my new business. But then came the rest of the news. The guy taking over the community John was building wanted to keep using me, and even better, John wanted us to join him with the new builder he was going to work for. This was our first-ever expansion! I had no idea what this meant for me, but he assured me that I could become a subcontractor at the new company as well.

I didn't really know what to think. How was I going to work for two builders at the same time? I didn't spend much time contemplating it, because the trash was piling up. At the time, working in the two communities did not present a challenge, but later, the growing pains would really begin to show.

John told some of his new coworkers in a meeting that he had found a guy who would do cleanup and mowing, and that is when the word got out about my business. Over the next few weeks, although it felt like it happened instantly, more than thirty communities requested us for mowing, site cleanup, and other random tasks.

As we were mowing lots one day in one of these neighborhoods under construction, the site manager stopped me to ask if we could also pick up trash in his community. Without hesitating, I said yes. That triggered what seemed like an avalanche of work, because word went through Ryland Homes that they had a cleanup guy on their hands.

One of the construction managers asked me if I would be willing to sweep out some houses under construction.

I looked at him and said, "Sir, I would bathe your cat if you paid me to."

He laughed and then told me that most of the home buyers liked to stop by on the weekends to see the different stages of the houses being built. The only problem was, the houses were littered with boxes and trash and sawdust. That made the houses dangerous and unattractive to walk through. So we agreed to clean up and sweep out the houses to make them safer.

At that time, Ryland was building roughly eight hundred to nine hundred houses per year in Charlotte. We agreed on a rate of $75–150, depending on the house, for sweeping and cleaning.

It's not the person with the most resources who wins; it's the one who is the most resourceful. I learned that saying yes and being willing to solve a client's pain point, even if I didn't have the answer right away, was the key to success.

> **It's not the person with the most resources who wins; it's the one who is the most resourceful.**

In my experience, construction managers often had an incredibly long list of tasks to be completed but limited resources, and I realized that if I could step in, solve their issues, and make them look like the hero to their supervisors, I became indispensable. The more problems I solved, the more trust I built, and soon enough, my company was the go-to solution.

Resourcefulness creates opportunities, builds loyalty, and secures your place as an essential partner.

One of the construction managers later came to me complaining about always failing inspections on his water meters. Apparently, when it was time for a house to get a water meter that supplied water to the house from the city, the city inspector would come inspect the house to see if it was ready for the meter to be installed. If there was any dirt or water or debris in the subsurface water meter box, he would not approve the installation of the water meter but would charge them a fee for coming out.

> ✏ **ACTION:** Ask each of your clients what they need but can't seem to get help with. It might not be what you currently offer, but you never know what it may lead to. Helping with your customers' biggest pain point will help you become a superhero in their eyes.
>
> _____
>
> _____
>
> _____
>
> _____
>
> _____

Most homes were not being approved for water meters due to debris in the water meter box, which was causing a problem because they needed water to get final approval. We began to clean and prepare the water meter boxes for the inspection. This provided yet another source of revenue on almost every house.

Ryland Homes had thirty-two communities in Charlotte at that time. We mowed home lots at thirty dollars each, swept houses for a hundred each on average, and cleaned water meter boxes in those same communities. I didn't realize it at the time, but we were diversified! When mowing was done, there was still plenty of work, and builders were selling homes daily—the housing market was booming!

· · · · ·

Transactions lead to more transactions—so always say yes! Don't wait for the perfect, glamorous work to come your way. Accept any type of job, and then find ways to turn it into something valuable. If you're willing to solve people's problems—whether it's cleaning up trashy sites, mowing overgrown grass, or cleaning dirty houses—they will pay you and want you around. The key is to turn those opportunities into something profitable.

I learned that money is everywhere if you're willing to listen to your customers. Often, they'll ask for something outside your usual scope. The mistake many business owners make is responding with, "No, we don't do that." What a lost opportunity! If I had said that, I would have missed out on building an eight-figure erosion control business. Seize every opportunity, solve every problem, and watch your business grow.

✎ **ACTION:** Write down two new solutions that you could provide for your current clients and present them at your next interaction. Remember, Apple supplied the personal computer, but then went on to add music, communications, entertainment, and financing. Be ready to expand your services!

_____

_____

_____

_____

_____

5

LESSONS FROM THE FIELD
Hiring, Hustling, and Holding On

One of the hardest things I learned early on is that hiring is painful. I think I made every mistake in the book—and maybe a couple more mistakes that could be scribbled in the margin! I hired a couple of guys from the gym, thinking, *These guys work out, so they must be motivated and in good shape.* Boy, was I wrong.

They only liked to work out. I mistook doing a set on the bench press and resting for five minutes as being willing to work hard.

I hired people from church, only to find out that their definition of *hard work* did not match mine. Of course, that made my experience at church the following weeks very awkward. I learned to never hire from church. I also learned that if someone from church has "been looking for a job for months," that is not because the good Lord was saving them for me! No one who is a hard worker and actually wants to get a job is "looking for a job for months" in a booming market.

We also hired family members. Bad idea. Hiring family members is usually about convenience, not about finding the best person for the job.

Looking back, most of my hardest times in business came from hiring decisions I made. This is where I hurt the most people and where I got hurt the most.

Hiring is one of the toughest parts of running a business—and it always will be. Over time, I learned the hard way that you must hire slowly and fire quickly. Every time I rushed a hire out of desperation, it led to problems—without exception. It wasn't just poor work performance that caused issues; it was character flaws that stood out the most. People with integrity and drive can overcome skill gaps, but those with weak character will drag your team down and create lasting damage. When I spotted those character flaws, I knew it was time to part ways, no matter how hard it seemed in the moment.

One of the most valuable lessons I learned is that great workers attract other great workers. People with high standards surround themselves with others who share their work ethic. Leaders in particular have the ability to bring in top talent if you create an environment that inspires them. When you find someone with leadership qualities, hire them—they'll draw in more people like them, and that can transform your team.

I also realized that recruiting is a constant process. You should always be recruiting, no matter where you are. Whether I was at the gas station, the grocery store, or on a jobsite, I always kept my eyes open for potential talent. You never know where you might find someone who can make a real difference in your business.

> *You never know where you might find someone who can make a real difference in your business.*

Build your team with intentionality. Surround yourself with people of character and skill, and your business will thrive. Don't settle for mediocrity, because the strength of your team directly impacts the success of your business.

Tracy showed up one day in the middle of the week, brought me lunch, and said, "I quit my job." She was sad—a situation at work had made her very uncomfortable. So she quit. I couldn't believe my ears. I was upset about the situation, but I was also upset because this was the only paycheck we had that was a regular income.

> ✐ **ACTION:** Take a few minutes and list three or four character traits that are nonnegotiable for future employees. Keep this list handy and never hire anyone that doesn't fulfill all these traits!
>
> _____
>
> _____
>
> _____
>
> _____
>
> _____

I always thought a weekly paycheck was safe. The problem with that is that these "safe" paychecks don't just fall from heaven. No, people write and sign those checks, and you never know what those people are thinking or what they are about to do.

The solution came pretty quickly: We had way too much work to do and not enough people to do it, so Tracy took a couple of the employees and led a crew herself. Now we were a two-crew operation. She had worked with me so much that she already knew what to do.

On days when the jobs were so big that I needed all the guys to help, Tracy would run and get materials. By this time, we had started installing grass seed and laying our straw mats to hold down the seed so it could germinate. The straw mats were one hundred feet long and rolled up tight like a cigar. The rolls were nine feet long, about twelve inches wide, and thirty pounds each.

We had a Dodge Intrepid as our family car, and I was driving the truck. Tracy would take our car to the material supplier, and they would load her up. She would return looking like she was driving the Griswolds' station wagon in *Christmas Vacation*. Jeff at Green Resource still laughs today as he tells the story of loading up ten-foot-wide straw mats on top of the car and tying them down with her windows open, then filling the trunk with a half-ton of grass seed and fertilizer and wishing her luck. The car was almost ten feet tall with this load! When she arrived on the jobsite, she was smiling from ear to ear, and man, let me tell you—she had stories from the trip!

Suddenly, as non-glorious as our profession was, we had construction managers in thirty-two communities waiting for their turn for us to show up. There was only a handful of us—me, several guys, and, of course, Tracy.

On days when we mowed vacant lots, I would ride the tractor and Tracy would run the Weed eater. These were twelve-hour days back-to-back.

One day, I hit a curb with the front tire of my tractor, which resulted in a bent rim that made the tire go flat.

We took the tire off and took it to my grandmother's house. I got out the sledgehammer and started whaling on the rim. I became ever more frustrated because we were getting really far behind on work.

As I hammered away on the rim, sweat pouring off me, my grandmother came out and said, "Phillip, would you please stop this and go get a job like everyone else?"

On the inside, that devastated me, but I didn't have time to dwell on it. I told her that this was what I was supposed to do. That was really tough for me to hear from her, but as I look back, I am sure she was just worried about me. I eventually reshaped the rim somewhat and reseated the tire, filled it with air, and we were back in business!

• • • • •

Just because someone loves you doesn't mean they're giving you the right advice. One of the hardest lessons I learned was that even well-meaning people—those who love you and want the best for you—aren't always qualified to guide you in every area of life. It's important to make sure the person giving advice truly understands the field or challenge you're facing before you take it to heart. Often, advice that comes from a place of love can still hold you back. What's more, not everyone will believe in your vision or see the potential you do.

Don't let others project limitations onto you. When people doubt your dream, it's usually a reflection of their own fears, not your ability. If you know deep down what you're meant to do, you owe it to yourself to pursue it relentlessly. Trust your instincts and get after it with everything you've got. The only person who truly needs to believe in your vision is you.

> ✍ **ACTION:** Write out how you will handle it when someone doesn't believe in your vision. It will happen, so plan for how you will handle it now. How will you handle it gracefully?
>
> _____
>
> _____
>
> _____
>
> _____
>
> _____
>
> _____

On days when there was no Weed eater work to do or after she was already finished, Tracy would climb up on the fender of the tractor, sitting just over the enormous left rear tire, and ride with me while I mowed for hours at a time. We would bounce along together, and as I would make turns, she would lean into the turn as if she were riding a motorcycle. We would laugh as things would play out—like if the Bush Hog hit a big dirt clod or rock.

This was our only time spent together, because when we got home, it was cooking and cleaning and bills from 8:00 to 10:00 p.m. Then we would go to bed and start all over again the next morning. Looking back, riding together on the tractor was not very safe, but we knew we were doing what we were supposed to do . . . and we were doing it together.

6

OPPORTUNITIES AND OVERWHELM

Learning to Navigate Growth

I originally feared John's move to a competing home-builder would be the death of my young business. Little did I know that that transition would turn out to be the rocket fuel that really got my business off the ground and shot us into a whole other realm of opportunity.

John went to work for an even busier homebuilder named Pulte Homes, which had built one thousand homes per year in Charlotte. I started working in John's new Pulte community in addition to his previous Ryland Homes community. We were so busy that it never even occurred to me to fill out the sub-contractor agreement and other necessary documents to legitimately work on these new jobsites. A couple of months later, I asked John about payment for the work I had been doing at Pulte, and he realized he had forgotten to fill out the paperwork on his end too! It was quite frowned upon to work on a site without being officially contracted, so we had to get that straightened out.

By this time, we had started mowing and picking up trash in a number of other Pulte communities as well. Plus, we'd recently been introduced to a local developer who hired us to pick up trash in a massive new development they were building. This company was clearing and developing a huge tract of land, roughly two thousand acres, which they'd then sell as lots or even whole sections to different builders. They needed help picking up the trash left over from their own crews and also mowing the lots.

One day, the land developer met up with me and asked if I could install a walking trail. He said there was not much to it—just chop down enough trees to make a ten-foot-wide walking trail. The only catch was, there were a couple of ravines that would need footbridges constructed to cross the twenty-foot-deep ravines. He then asked, "Do you have access to a skid steer?"

"Sure!" I told him. "No problem. We can get this trail in."

A skid steer is a piece of heavy equipment that has many uses, but it is mainly used in construction site grading. I had driven a friend's skid steer before . . . but not more than one hundred feet. I got the number of the local Caterpillar salesman from a friend and told him I wanted to talk about buying or renting a skid steer. He delivered one the next day for me to try out.

I also had zero experience building bridges. Fortunately, I had a friend at church, Matt, who was a deck builder, so I reached out to him for advice on building footbridges. Matt also had a small business— and what's more, he even owned a skid steer!

He agreed to work with me on the project and got started building the bridges. One was roughly twelve feet long, and the other was much longer at twenty feet, so it had to have an upright post in the middle for support that was seated deep into the ravine. Matt was very meticulous, and I knew he would overbuild them and that they would look awesome. He did not disappoint. Within a month, we had the trail installed—complete with bridges—and turned it over to the developer.

· · · · ·

If you're open to opportunities, the possibilities are endless. The key to growth is a willingness to seize opportunities and solve problems, even when they fall outside your comfort zone. I expanded to two major clients by simply being eager to address their pain points and adjusting my approach. By moving

NO COLLEGE, NO PROBLEM

with John to Pulte Homes and then diversifying with a developer, I discovered that being flexible opened doors I never imagined.

If you're open to opportunities, the possibilities are endless.

I wasn't a bridge builder, but I knew that to land the walking trail job, I needed to find someone who was. Don't limit yourself to what you know—find strategic partners who can fill the gaps and help you expand. Building strong relationships and being resourceful will create opportunities you wouldn't have thought possible.

As we grew, we started struggling financially because adding employees and working them such long hours grew the payroll astronomically. The customers were supposed to pay within 30 days, but for various reasons, a lot of invoices stretched out to 90–120 days. Some were even 150 days.

I knew things were tight, and I was the shock absorber in the whole thing. The employees had to be paid weekly, and the customers were slow paying at best.

One evening, I had dinner with my grandparents to catch up, and they asked how things were going. I told them it was promising but tough. I wasn't even sure how I was going to afford gas for the trucks the next week. I was completely out of money.

> ✎ **ACTION:** The walking trail project was far more technical than I was accustomed to, but we figured it out. Take a minute to think back on the opportunities you've had, and list two projects you have declined due to their complexity. Write out how you could complete them now. Then reach back out to the customer—it might not be too late!
>
> _____
>
> _____
>
> _____
>
> _____
>
> _____
>
> _____

My grandfather loaned money to me for diesel fuel and urged me to go push the customers for payment. I was so grateful. It made dinner that night taste even better.

Tracy and I were working all these jobs by day, and then at night, Tracy cooked and took care of the house while I wrote out invoices by hand for everything.

What made the invoicing so much work was the fact that in each community, there were roughly thirty houses under construction on any given day. Some communities had closer to fifty houses, while others had as few as fifteen, depending on the community. The homebuilder considered each and every house lot a separate job, because that was how their profit models were built.

So if we went to one lot and installed ten feet of fencing, I would have to write a bill for ten feet, which totaled around $13.50. Then on the lot next door, we might install fifty feet, which would be another small invoice of $67.50. Some of the lots were only charged $6 or $7 depending on what was needed, so I would have to handwrite an invoice on their carbon copy invoices for each and every lot in all twenty-five or so communities.

If we performed other services like sweeping out the houses, we had to write a separate invoice for that because it required a different cost code. The other builder we had picked up wanted their invoices emailed, but it was the same process.

This amounted to hundreds if not thousands of invoices every week. Keeping up with them, tracking them, following up on them, and collecting payment on them were enormous challenges that kept me quite busy to say the least. Early on, I had to write only one or two invoices per day, which was easy, but as we slowly progressed, I was barely able to build my accounting skills fast enough to keep up with the growing business. I did keep up, but it would not be long before I hit a wall.

· · · · ·

Growth is exciting, but without proper planning, it can quickly turn into a financial nightmare. I learned this the hard way when I didn't take the time to plan for my business's growth. The thrill of expanding masked the fact that I was running out of cash. Worse yet, I had no policy in place to manage aging receivables, which eventually put me in a serious bind.

It wasn't until we implemented a weekly receivables meeting to track who was behind and plan to follow up on payments that things started to turn around. This became one of our most critical practices, allowing us to stay on top of cash flow and avoid future financial crises. Growth without cash flow is just a ticking time bomb. Make sure you track your receivables regularly, or the excitement of growth could lead you straight into a wall.

✏️ **ACTION:** Plan now for your growth! Will your current accounting practices scale well if you grow 20 percent next year? Take some time now and audit your current practices. Write two or three things that you need to change.

_____

_____

_____

_____

_____

_____

If you are feeling stuck and do not know what to change, I have found that a fresh set of eyes can be a game changer. Reach out today if you need some help breaking through that wall!

www.CoreBusinessEssentials.com

7

JULIO'S LESSON
Perseverance, Laughter, and
the Power of a Team

Outside of my family, Julio was one of my favorite people on earth. I still do not know how Julio came to join the team—he must have been a referral from someone. But even though we haven't worked together in fifteen years, he is in my top ten favorite people.

Julio is from Guatemala and worked harder than anyone I have ever met. He would work fourteen-hour days and still joke with me on the way home, while I was completely worn out. He was ten years older than me. He had this quirk where if either of us said something funny, he would laugh and take both of his hands, lift his hat straight up in the air about six inches above his head, and then set it back down. It was the funniest thing. I tried to make him laugh while we drove to jobsites just to see him do it, and then I would laugh even harder!

Ryland Homes somehow managed to hire three Johns who all managed sites on the south side of town. John W. was the one who put me into business. He is also the one who moved on to another builder that fueled our expansion. Then we were down to only two Johns, which I will explain later.

John H. scheduled us to come to his jobsite at Ryland where he built townhomes. That morning, he informed us that he had a problem with the footings on a townhome; the concrete guy had poured them too thick. He wanted us to chisel through a footing with a pickax and get it down about twelve inches where the power pole could come through.

After about an hour of taking turns swinging the pickax at the footing, the only thing we'd accomplished was sending a constant spray of concrete dust and debris flying in our faces. We weren't making any progress at all. It felt hopeless to me, and I got really annoyed. I told Julio, "I've got to go to the store. I can't take it. I'm quitting this jobsite."

Julio just looked at me and said, "Go to the store, Felipe."

I fumed the whole way to the store. I could not believe John had us on such a terrible project. I bought a drink for myself and one for Julio, and I decided at that point I was going to quit working for him. John

H. was impossible to work for. I was going to hang it up. I had made up my mind.

When I arrived at the jobsite, Julio said, "Hey, Felipe," and motioned me toward him.

I walked over and said, "Okay, Julio, let's get in the truck. We are quitting this guy."

He said, "No, Felipe, you don't understand. I got it!"

While I was gone, Julio had continued working by himself and chiseled away the concrete all the way through the footing. I could not believe it. This guy had just saved me from quitting this customer. Where I thought it was hopeless, he just kept digging in.

As I look back, there were probably a couple other times when Julio kept going when I was ready to quit. It was no mistake that God had paired me with this man.

I quit, but Julio didn't. He saved my company on the day I was ready to give up.

• • • • •

No one can succeed alone, so surround yourself with people who will carry you when you stumble. Everyone has down days and moments of exhaustion. It's during those times that the people you surround yourself with make all the difference. A strong support system isn't just helpful; it's essential. In business and in life, you need people who are in your corner, who will keep pushing forward when you're worn down, and who will pick you up when you need it most.

> *No one can succeed alone, so*
> *surround yourself with people who*
> *will carry you when you stumble.*

But it's not a one-way street; you must be there for them too. True success is built on relationships in which everyone gives and receives support. Remember, no one has ever made it far without a team. If you're aiming for long-term success, invest in building a circle of people who lift each other up through the highs and lows.

> ✐ **ACTION:** List two or three people who have been there for you. Take the time to make this list. Call them today and thank them. Also, make sure you take the time to be that person for others!
>
> _____
>
> _____
>
> _____
>
> _____

Each morning, Julio would ask what jobs were we going to do so he would know what supplies to load onto the truck. One morning, I said, "We have to go see John again. He needs a huge list of things taken care of prior to an inspection."

Julio looked at me and asked in Spanish, "The *gordo* or the *feo*?"

I looked at him, and we just stood there for what felt like ten seconds. I said, "What?"

"Which John?" he said. "The *gordo* or the *feo*?"

"Julio, I don't know what you are saying."

"*Gordo* means fat, Felipe."

"Oh, what is the other word?"

"The *feo*?"

"Yeah," I answered.

"Haha, Felipe, the ugly one."

"Oh, that's easy," I said. "We are going to see *Feo*!"

Twenty years later, I still belly laugh every time this story pops into my mind!

• • • • •

One day while picking up trash and sweeping out houses, a construction manager named Bill, who had become a good friend, handed me a pack of zip ties and asked me to tie up the silt fence at the bottom of the hill.

Silt fences are two-foot-high cloth fences that are anchored into the ground to slow water runoff from construction sites during massive rain events. I did not know it at the time, but this is the point where we took the very first step toward becoming an erosion control contractor, which would eventually lead us out of being just a company that provided jobsite labor.

I said, "Sure, Bill!"

Later that evening, I met Bill back in his job trailer to talk and go over my invoices. As we sat there, I saw a bill from his silt fence installer sitting on his desk. I remembered seeing that company come into the community earlier and install one of those silt fences. His invoice was for roughly $400, and they had been there an hour—if that!

So I asked Bill, "Can I tie up more of those fences for you?"

He said, "Sure, those guys are busier than they could ever handle anyway."

He told me about a fence he would need the following week, and man, was I excited! I went straight to Home Depot to get the materials. I found some cheap fence fabric, but I could not find the zip ties anywhere. I finally found some in the heating and air-conditioning department, but the problem was, they were each four feet long. I bought them anyway because I did not want to tell Bill that I couldn't do the job. We installed that silt fence with those gigantic zip ties. I never heard anything about the gigantic zip ties, and they certainly did the job, but it must have looked hilarious!

We started out installing silt fences with just me and a few guys using only picks and shovels. For the rest of the year, we dug six-inch-deep by six-inch-wide trenches around the sides and fronts of the yard of a house, installed the fabric fences, and filled the trenches back in. The four of us would dig anywhere from 500–1,500 feet of trenches each day. It was tough work, but in time, it would take my business in a totally new direction.

• • • • •

Surround yourself with people you enjoy at work. It will transform tough jobs into great experiences. Also, be ready and open. Chances are you are feet or inches from your game-changing opportunity. Bill asked me to tie up a fence. It seemed so insignificant at the time . . . until I saw that invoice on his desk. Now I can look back and see that this one request ended up changing my career and my life!

✎ **ACTION:** Before this day, silt fence repair was not even on my radar. It was just an item that my customer asked me to take care of on that particular day. Take a minute to write two or three things that you have been asked to do that could actually have potential. Grab a friend and have them think about it with you. It is surprising how often we quit inches from the goal line that we can't see!

_____

_____

_____

_____

_____

8

THE $1,000 BREAKTHROUGH
Embracing Change to Stay Ahead

eo John wanted to meet with me one day. As soon as we met, he blurted out, "Your invoices are killing me! All I do anymore is approve your invoices."

I said, "John, you are the one who asked me to do all this work. Do you want me to not bill you?"

"No," he said. "Just give me one price for each lot, and that's it. I can't take dozens of invoices for each little task. I want one bill for each house, period."

This excited me and scared me to death at the same time. What if we used up more materials and time than what the new lump sum was? What if I went bankrupt? How was I supposed to know how much to charge? Back then, I didn't keep up with this on a computer.

I said, "John, if the price is wrong, I could go out of business. I don't even know how to come up with a single price for the fencing."

All I knew was that I charged two dollars per linear foot, and I installed as much fencing as was needed, sometimes five feet, sometimes one hundred, and other times up to four hundred.

He said, "Let's start at a thousand dollars per house and go from there. You are killing me with your five-dollar invoices. Your invoices are taking up my whole truck!"

That was a huge number! I tried my best to maintain my composure, and I think I mostly did, but when I got to my truck, I let it out. "A thousand dollars per house! Holy cow!" It felt like I had won the lottery!

We started this new process right away, although it was really rough at first. We installed fencing on a new house every couple of days for him. I would invoice by the new system once we started working on the lot. However, I also had to keep track of the houses under the old system on a notepad. It was tedious for me, but I could see the light at the end of the tunnel. I mentioned this system to the other jobsite managers, but none of them were impressed. Their bonuses were calculated by how much they came in under budget on each house.

They did still complain, as John had previously, about my having too many invoices. This was confusing to me because they were the ones asking me to break down every bit of our work on the invoices. Yet they still complained.

John was wise and didn't want to trade his spare time for coding hundreds of invoices per week. Little did I know, he had someone in the office run a report to find out how much he was spending for erosion control on average on each house, and that was how he came up with the $1,000 per house. So that means the other managers were willing to code hundreds of my invoices per week in hopes that they could get a few bucks more per house, going against the long-term data that their own company had been collecting.

After a while, each of the homebuilders hired a purchasing manager, and they eventually brought me into the office to negotiate a new lump sum on every lot in every community. This was scary and awesome at the same time.

· · · · ·

Be creative with your billing and systems—it could unlock new levels of freedom in your business. While this particular breakthrough wasn't mine, but John's, it changed everything for both of us. One of the biggest mistakes businesses make is sticking with the same systems, like invoicing, without adapting them as they scale. What worked when you were small might not work when you're handling multiple clients or projects. Most processes don't scale well, and if you're not careful, outdated systems can hold you back.

Make it a habit to audit your processes regularly, especially during periods of heavy growth. At least twice a year, step back and assess whether your systems still fit the current size and demands of your business. Don't hesitate to bring in someone with fresh eyes to evaluate where improvements can be made. If your processes haven't changed in a year or two, there's a good chance they need to be modified. Evolving your systems is key to sustaining long-term growth.

Evolving your systems is key to sustaining long-term growth.

🖉 **ACTION:** Tell someone who is ahead of you in business about your current systems. Ask if they can recommend an upgrade.

_____

_____

_____

_____

John's frustration would eventually turn us into a high-tech erosion control contractor. Luckily, I had data for this, and I was ready when I was called into the office. I was keeping up with the profitability of each lot. The problem was, I had been manually tracking profitability for each project in a spiral notebook, and I needed a faster way to analyze profits because it was taking up nearly my whole day.

My uncle suggested using Excel, and that day, he taught me how to use spreadsheets and built a page full of formulas that would change the process forever. I'll admit I was resistant to technology and Excel in the beginning, but within just a few weeks, I had more data than my competitors available to me in an instant!

In fact, within the first month, I had more data about the house lots I worked on than my customers, the developers, did—at least about erosion control. This new lump sum for the house lots put me way ahead of the competition. All the competitors were reluctant to consider the lump-sum pricing and downright refused, but with the data I had, I knew which house lots made more money and which house lots were a guaranteed loss. I also knew which managers were more profitable for me and who the better managers were. This helped me schedule and know who to prioritize.

Later, after I brought a CFO aboard, we would have incredible amounts of data that showed us how many minutes each truck would run, how many minutes our machines would run, how long each house lot took, which crew was the fastest at which type of site—and the list goes on.

. . . . .

Data is one of the major keys to profits, and embracing technology is essential to staying ahead of the competition. We were accumulating mountains of data every day, and if I hadn't taken the time to learn how to use spreadsheets and other tools, I would have fallen behind. That knowledge gave me a critical edge over the competition.

Today, technology is evolving even faster, with AI and other advancements reshaping industries. If you're not staying ahead of the curve, you'll fall behind. Always be on the lookout for new tools and improvements that can streamline your business and increase profitability.

Beyond technology, always be ready to listen and learn. Be open to meeting people, sharing your ideas, and absorbing life-changing advice. Never be too busy to hear the insights that could save you time, energy, and resources. Sometimes, the right advice at the right time can give you back the most valuable resource of all: your time.

> ✎ **ACTION:** If you are not tech savvy, find someone who is *today*. It's one of the best investments you can make. Technology pays off when you take the time to master it or hire the right people who can.
>
> _____
>
> _____
>
> _____
>
> _____
>
> _____
>
> _____

And here's the thing—none of that requires a college degree. I didn't need a classroom to teach me how to listen, learn, or take action. No professor handed me the skills that got me ahead. I built them by showing up, working hard, and figuring things out along the way. I've met plenty of people with degrees who are still stuck, waiting for the right opportunity because college didn't necessarily teach them how to create one. A diploma might open some doors, but it doesn't guarantee success. Skills, work ethic, and the ability to solve real problems do. And those aren't necessarily things you can learn in a classroom.

9

NAVIGATING TIGHTROPES
*Payment Challenges,
Persistence, and Progress*

I n construction, payment terms are a tough thing
to deal with. Sometimes, construction managers
would sit on the invoices for months before signing
them to be paid, which only then triggered the
thirty-day payment process. This was very frustrating
and resulted in our getting paid an average of sixty-
three days after invoicing.

This kept Tracy and me on quite a tight budget.
We just assumed that the invoices would be paid, and
we had to learn how to navigate this process since we
were new in business and didn't want to rock the boat.
It became a tightrope walk because I had never learned
how to negotiate for payment. I began to reach out

to the site managers individually, and their replies all seemed to be the same: "I will get to it. We are just super busy right now."

I thought, *I am pretty busy too.*

I figured out that in-person visits about aging invoices were far more effective than just making phone calls, but I knew that at our current rate of growth, that would be unsustainable. So I began giving preferential treatment and faster scheduling to the communities that paid sooner, and I began to slow the service to the communities that paid slower. I also spoke to the area managers above the site managers about the problem. Both of these methods worked and helped out quite a bit, but it was not flawless.

✐ ACTION: Write two ways to improve your collections process today!

_____

_____

_____

_____

_____

· · · · ·

In 2005, while we were on-site taking care of the erosion control needs and cleanup, one of the construction managers gave the crew and me some large shop brooms and asked us to sweep the street where big piles of dirt had been dumped. We started sweeping the streets with brooms weekly in several communities. I asked the construction manager if he would be interested in having them swept by a truck weekly, and he said, "Absolutely!"

I went to the bank where we had our account and asked the bank branch manager for a loan for a street sweeper. We sat down with Harvey at the local regional bank, and he asked how long we had been in business. Of course, since we were in a small town, he already knew the answer. He was one of the nicest people in town, loved by all. The truck I had picked out was in California, and the price tag was $102,000 plus delivery.

He said, "Phillip, I just can't." Looking back on the situation now and remembering his face and demeanor, I think he was as sad to turn us down as I was to be turned down.

I did not plead with him because I could tell that it was not the answer he was wanting to give either. No money, no education, no real business history, and wanting a huge loan on a huge truck . . . that is a tough combination. I couldn't blame him, but I knew I was supposed to start sweeping these neighborhood streets. It was an obvious new offering for my business. I could feel it!

I kept on searching and finally found exactly what I needed in Washington State. It was bigger, uglier, older, and farther away, but it was still a street sweeper. This one was only $30,000, so I had hit the jackpot!

We ordered the truck, and we were in the sweeping business. This truck was more or less utilitarian. It was a 1983 city street sweeper. The front tires were foam-filled and not quite round. They were more egg-shaped from the truck sitting unused for so long. The tires bounced like crazy everywhere we went because they were so misshaped. On the good nights, the tires bounced in unison! We were not pretty, but we were sweeping and creating a new normal in construction.

· · · · ·

Spend only what's necessary to get the job done—especially when you're proving a concept. Too many people dive headfirst into financing everything for a new idea, only to realize later that the concept doesn't work or isn't nearly as profitable as they imagined during their initial excitement. It's easy to dream big but expensive to fail big. If you're testing a new concept, start small. Prove it works before you pour all your resources into it.

*It's easy to dream big but
expensive to fail big.*

Before going all in, start small—test, adjust, and refine your aim. Taking measured shots first allows you to minimize risk, sharpen your approach, and ensure that when it's time to go big, you're firing with precision and confidence. Don't let enthusiasm blind you—small, calculated steps will take you further than a leap without proof.

> ✎ **ACTION:** Take some time now to write down how you can start that new product/service line inexpensively, possibly by renting or buying used to prove the concept and gain cash flow.
>
> _____
>
> _____
>
> _____
>
> _____
>
> _____

Friday nights became "quality time night" for Tracy and me. Just us and the street sweeper. We found that we could sweep twelve communities in fourteen hours. We got paid $280 per community, so we were killing it! It made for long days, and most of the time, we would split up the workload between Friday nights and Saturday nights. Before long, we had both Friday and Saturday nights filled up, sweeping twenty-plus communities per weekend.

We eventually ended up sweeping more than forty communities weekly and had to hire additional drivers to help with the workload. The beauty of the street sweeper was that it was good for the environment. The process before we started sweeping was that the builders used street washers. The builders would pay huge water trucks to blast all the dirt, mud, and debris down the street drains that led to the creek. These contaminants and all the mud were filling in our local creeks that led directly to our lake, which was our city's water supply. The street sweeper cleaned all of that out of the street and dumped it on-site so that it could be dealt with appropriately without blasting it into our lake.

The big sweeper eventually broke down to the point of no return, but we had saved up enough by this point to trade it in and finally get a loan on that newer street sweeper that I had originally wanted. Now we were cooking with gas. Now we had round tires, heat, a quiet ride, a CD player—the works. Date night was upgraded from here on out!

10

BALANCING BUSINESS AND LIFE

The Power of Focus and
Fresh Perspectives

I n late 2005, it became obvious that our path to success was going to be erosion control. Even though we had started out picking up trash and completing various tasks, our future was in silt fence and erosion control. It would be easier to hire for it and would get us away from a paid hourly rate. Plus, it was in extremely high demand, and there was almost no one competing against us.

At this point, we knew that erosion control and silt fencing were our future. Erosion had become a big problem, and it was getting exponentially worse.

It affected everyone. Whether on beaches, dunes, or construction projects, erosion control devices are used to protect our water supply.

Silt fences were created to wrap around areas (including construction sites) where the soil is bare. Each time it rained on a construction site, prior to silt fencing, the mud would run off the site, flow down the street, enter the street drains, and then reach the creek. At that point, the mud would settle out of the water, and a pile of sediment would form in the center of the creek.

As the creeks filled with sediment, it would kill all the wildlife and aquatic life from fish to snails. The streams would divert to new areas and begin a new series of erosion, which would push sediment into the lakes. The silt fence is the first line of defense from all of this. It lets the rain run off the site but holds the sediment back to prevent this devastating process.

This led to some tough conversations with the site managers, because they wanted me to continue picking up trash and sweeping out the houses, but we just did not have enough human resources to do both. It took a couple of months to totally drop the other tasks that had given the business its start, but soon, we were solely an erosion-control contractor.

Amazon started as an online book retailer. Play-Doh was first sold as a wallpaper cleaner. Apple began with personal computers and evolved into a global leader in consumer electronics. These companies succeeded because they weren't afraid to adapt, refine their focus, and let go of what wasn't core to their vision. Sometimes growth comes from focusing on what you do best.

Sometimes growth comes from focusing on what you do best.

• • • • •

Take a step back and evaluate your business. Are there products or services that could become your entire core focus? Is there something you're offering that has more potential than you've realized? Don't be afraid to streamline and concentrate on what will drive your business forward. Like Amazon, Play-Doh, and Apple, focusing on the right thing can lead to massive success.

The high demand and low supply for erosion-control contractors quickly caused us to hit the limit of how many fences we were able to install. I needed some help and spoke to a friend who, fortunately, was looking for additional work because his business had been slow. I reached out to Matt, who had built the bridges for me earlier, and told him about how busy we were. So he came on temporarily to help out.

✐ **ACTION:** Write down every product and service that you currently offer. Reassess and determine if each one still fits today. There is a high probability that some of the products/services do not belong anymore, even if they were part of the offering that gave you your start.

_____

_____

_____

_____

_____

_____

We were still excavating the trenches with picks and shovels at that time. After his first week, Matt came up to me and said, "I have been thinking . . . why don't we try renting a trencher? I found some for rent and want to try it."

A trencher! For the whole year, I had been trying to dig trenches faster and never even considered a trencher. He rented a walk-behind trenching machine called a Dingo, which was similar to a walk-behind lawn mower. The next day, it felt like a whole new world had opened up. I could not believe that I had not thought of this.

I was so busy working in my environment that I hadn't stopped to ask if I was actually using the best practices. It took someone from the outside less than a week to spot a more efficient way of doing things—something I had missed for months.

This taught me an important lesson: Always get advice, especially when you're in the thick of things. You don't have to take every piece of advice, but as your business grows, you need guidance to keep up with that growth.

When you're in the trenches, it's hard to see the whole battlefield. Fresh eyes can reveal opportunities and solutions you might never have noticed. Don't wait until you're stuck to seek help—get advice early and often. It could save you time, money, and unnecessary frustration.

In 2006, when our third child was born, Tracy stepped away from her leadership role to focus on being at home with the baby. This transition required her to take on a new role—not as a leader in a business but as the spouse of a business owner. This left a gaping hole in the business because we didn't have anyone to fill her role in the company.

As we spoke with our peers, we discovered that many of their spouses faced similar struggles. The truth is, entrepreneurship is tough—and so is being married to an entrepreneur. There are no set hours, no turning off the lights at the end of the day—it's like having another baby that demands attention at all hours.

> ✐ **ACTION:** Today, find someone ahead of you in business and tell them about your current business and struggles. People generally love to help. Ask someone to visit your place of work. The ideas from this will almost always bring about change.
>
> _____
>
> _____
>
> _____
>
> _____
>
> _____

Owning a business is an incredible journey, offering freedoms and income opportunities that aren't typically available in a standard workplace. But while the entrepreneurial life can be rewarding, being the spouse of an entrepreneur can be just as tough as running a business.

It can feel isolating at times, as the demands of the business often pull the entrepreneur away. Leadership doesn't stop at business; it extends to your homelife as well. As an entrepreneur, it's crucial to ensure your spouse feels fulfilled and supported, with their own outlets for growth and connection.

· · · · ·

It's easy to get lost in the demands of the business, but making space for your spouse's needs is essential for a thriving relationship. Luckily, there are resources, like podcasts and communities, specifically designed to help entrepreneurs and their spouses navigate this unique journey together. Remember, your business can't thrive if your homelife is struggling. Leadership is about balance.

✐ **ACTION:** Take your spouse to dinner. Ask them for two or three ways you can make their life easier living with an entrepreneur. No matter how well you have it together, it takes a lot to live with a business owner. Have a dinner date this week to talk about it!

_____

_____

_____

_____

_____

_____

11

THE POWER OF SHOWING UP
Building More Than a Business

So far, our big claim to fame was that we showed up every day, were on time, and would do everything that no one else would do. By this time, the housing boom was in full swing and had been booming from 2004 to 2007. We hired a few more people and had moved away from hiring friends and family. Our workload was only desirable to people who *really* needed the work. This was hard work and very labor intensive.

I was still running a crew myself. Matt's business began to gain traction again, so he went on to build that further. We had also hired a couple more people and put them in leadership positions to lead Tracy's previous crew, which was a relief to Tracy and me.

By the peak in 2007, we had ten employees—just ten people handling an operation that felt twice that size. It somehow seemed like both a lot and not nearly enough at the same time. We were stretched thin, juggling multiple projects, racing from one jobsite to the next, and doing whatever it took to keep up with demand. Each person wore multiple hats, jumping between roles to make sure the work got done. Some days, it felt like an unstoppable machine. Other days, it felt like we were barely holding it together. Either way, we kept pushing forward.

My accountant showed me we had billed more than $950,000 in 2006 alone! We were so busy doing the work every day that I had no idea what the numbers were. I never dreamed we would be just short of $1 million in revenue after only three years!

Transactions lead to more transactions—and sometimes, success comes from saying yes to the jobs no one else wants.

In just three years, my business had transformed from picking up trash to generating seven figures. The key? Being willing to take on the unglamorous, "unsexy" jobs that others overlooked. Success doesn't always start with the shiny opportunities; it often begins with humble, hard work.

Success doesn't always start with the shiny opportunities; it often begins with humble, hard work.

Another crucial element was knowing when to ask for help and seek advice. You don't have to know everything yourself—learning from others can accelerate your growth. Sometimes, it's the willingness to do the small, gritty tasks and seek guidance that paves the way to big success. I built a $1 million business in just three years—something no classroom could have taught me. The real keys were recognizing opportunities and having the drive to act on them. School can unlock a door, but many graduates get stuck in thinking that a degree automatically opens it for them. Success doesn't come from a diploma alone; it comes from taking initiative, seizing opportunities, and putting in the work to turn them into something real.

As we scaled up, I ran into logistical problems. Each of the communities I worked in was requesting us at the same time. This was really causing a problem because all the different communities would want us on the same day, but many of the communities were an hour apart on different sides of Charlotte, North Carolina. I was trying to please everyone, but in the process, I was pleasing no one. I had to come up with a plan—which was not popular at first but eventually proved to be very efficient and successful.

The plan was to divide the Charlotte metro area into quadrants and assign each quadrant to a specific day, then assign a day of the week to each quadrant. If a customer was scheduled for a Monday but did not provide an appropriate work list by the previous Friday, they had to wait until the following Monday for service.

> ✎ **ACTION:** Sometimes we are not good at realizing how far we have come. Take a few minutes to write about your workload from your first week in business. What was your revenue? Then, write where you are today. It is important to look back and be grateful for how far you have come. We business owners forget to celebrate the wins.
>
> _____
>
> _____
>
> _____
>
> _____
>
> _____
>
> _____

This caused the site managers to condense their lists of requests, which made us more efficient.

Sometimes the customer doesn't know what they really need—and that's where you come in.

In my experience, customers can have scattered ideas and incomplete lists of what they want done, which only leads to chaos and unmet expectations. They don't always take the time to think through the best approach, and that's when it's your job as a leader to step up. It's not enough to just do what they ask; sometimes, you have to guide them toward a better solution that they didn't even realize they needed.

As Henry Ford said, "If I had asked people what they wanted, they would have said faster horses." Your job is to see beyond what they're asking for and give them the solution that's truly going to work. That's how you build real value and trust.

> ✐ **ACTION:** If meeting with clients is an inefficient process, begin to script out how long the process should take. Thinking this through and writing it down will build a plan to recapture some of your time.
>
> _____
>
> _____
>
> _____
>
> _____
>
> _____

• • • • •

One day, a letter came in the mail from the IRS. I was being audited. Tracy and I did not sleep much that night worrying about the audit.

It turned out our charitable giving had triggered the audit. Up until this point, we had been paying a tithe to the local church on our gross revenues, not our profit, which caused our giving to look way outside the norm, especially since it had seemingly exploded over just a few years. It did not take much to prove our case, and the audit wrapped up almost as fast as it began. Whew!

We were able to continue tithing on the gross revenue until later in 2007 when we officially changed to tithing off the net pay. I approached the pastor to relay the information that there would be a large reduction in tithe. This probably was not standard practice, but the church was on a high growth trajectory, and he was thankful for the heads-up. It was a tough transition for me mentally to begin to tithe on the business profit instead of revenue, but it was needed because we couldn't sustain what we'd been doing.

During this time, our church upgraded facilities due to many people giving sacrificially, and we were so happy to have helped that. What an awesome experience to have played a big part in the changing of so many lives through new facilities. Tracy often jokes about how great it was that we gave so much that we triggered an IRS audit! We didn't spend much on ourselves and held our earnings loosely, so we had plenty to give and to share.

Always be ready and willing to give because success isn't just about the money you make; it's about the difference you make in people's lives.

Stacking up piles of cash for yourself feels good for a while, but it doesn't compare to the reward of investing in others. There are plenty of billionaires who have all the money they could ever want, but they're miserable. As a business leader, you have the power to change the trajectory of people's lives, not just through how you lead but through how you give.

• • • • •

When you lead with purpose and give intentionally, you're not just running a business; you're building a legacy. Lead with a mission that's bigger than personal gain, because at the end of the day, the impact you make on others will be far more fulfilling than the size of your bank account.

✍ **ACTION:** Decide today what percentage you will give to charity. It is easier to decide early on, when you are not earning as much. This can't wait. This should be one of the things you are most proud of. When your business is well-established, give not just your money but also your time. The world needs action-oriented leaders helping out in charities and churches as well.

_____

_____

_____

_____

_____

_____

12

CUTTING EGO AND COSTS AND GROWING WISE
The Hard Lesson of 2008

In 2007, the housing market began slowing down. No one knew it but the economy was about to hit a brick wall. I noticed that the workload started slowing down around August, so I started reaching out to the construction managers. Their response was that everything was fine and that they were about to start building an incredible number of houses. They were just on hold.

Each week, I called them, but I received the same response.

In November, one construction manager finally told me that a message had just come from their corporate office: "No more houses for the foreseeable future." By this time, I had exhausted quite a bit of our savings keeping all our employees on the payroll, thinking that work was just around the corner.

The next day, a project manager reached out to me and told me the new situation. I had two options: I could either accept a 20 percent price cut immediately and keep getting all their work . . . or I could refuse the 20 percent cut but lose all their work to my competitor.

This was the last builder we were still working for. All the work for the other builders had dried up. So I took the 20 percent cut. My competitor did not.

We survived, but now that I had taken a cut, I had to make cuts of my own.

Looking back, I think I can distill the lesson of that moment into one simple-to-understand but very hard-to-do principle: *Never let ego or pride get in the way of making smart decisions—especially when things are going well.*

During the housing boom, money was pouring in, everything was profitable, and egos were out of control. People were riding high, thinking the good times would never end. But when the money dried up, those who didn't keep their egos in check were the first to fall. I saw guys lose it all—bankruptcy, alcoholism, you name it—because they let pride lead them straight into trouble.

No matter how successful things look right now, you have to stay humble. The success that comes easily can disappear just as quickly. Pride will cloud your judgment and make you think you're invincible, but it can also be the very thing that takes you down. Keep your ego in check and stay grounded in humility and wisdom. Those are the tools that will carry you through both the good times and the bad.

No matter how successful things look right now, you have to stay humble.

☑ **ACTION:** What is the current environment telling you today? Listen hard. Write down a couple of first moves you would make if trouble started to surface in the economy or in your particular area of business. Write it down so you are not reacting in the moment.

_____

_____

_____

_____

_____

_____

In November 2007, due to all our work disappearing, we had to let all our employees go except for Julio. Unfortunately, one of those now-former employees was my cousin, which was really painful for both of us.

I remember being on jobsites and seeing the higher-level corporate employees of the homebuilder show up to a community. They would summon the construction manager and walk into their office. Then I would see the construction manager go to their truck and drive away, having just been told they lost their job. It was tough to see.

One Friday, we showed up to turn in our weekly bills to Patricia at Ryland, who we'd always enjoyed chatting and laughing with. But this time, there was no smiling face to greet us. Instead, there was only a telephone and note that read, "Please leave bills here at the desk. We will get them." Patricia had worked there for more than ten years and was loved by all the subcontractors, and she was replaced with a phone and a notepad.

The year 2008 was a slow slog. Julio and I worked one or two days per week for the year. That was all there was to do, but we felt fortunate because we heard of engineers who were now working at grocery stores and in fast food, trying to do anything they could to pay the bills.

Since we had slowed down enough to catch our breath, I went over to my pastor's house one day; we lived in the same community. I had questions about finances, and I finally had time to ask them. I asked him how much I should be saving and how to start investing for retirement.

He answered, "There is a guy named Dave Ramsey. Listen to him, and he should answer most of your questions."

Dave Ramsey—I had never heard of him. I went home and streamed his show while I was doing my computer work. People would call in and ask their personal finance questions, and he would answer them. Sometimes, if they did not want his advice, he would either call them out for their stupid behavior or he would say, "Well, you called me!"

It was entertaining. I was learning about new situations, many of which did not apply to me, but the interesting thing was, as I talked to other people, they had questions similar to what the callers were asking—and now I had the answers! It was a pretty cool experience. Tracy and I had questions of our own, but I didn't want to try to call and get through on the show, so we hired a Dave Ramsey Certified Financial Master Coach at the steep cost of two hundred dollars.

As the coach taught us the principles, Tracy and I got to know the coach better. When our paid time was up, they kept teaching us. The coach turned out to be a great friend and mentor. We received way more than two hundred dollars' worth of advice.

After the coaching program ended, we took Dave's class, *Financial Peace University*. This was backward from the norm, as most people took the class first and then hired a coach, but we seem to do most everything backward.

The class was a complete road map already laid out for us. Baby Step 1, Baby Step 2, Baby Step 3, and on up through Baby Step 7. First, you would save $1,000 in a starter emergency fund (Baby Step 1), and then you would pay off all your debt except your house (Baby Step 2). No planning was involved; we just had to follow the steps. Where I grew up, most people considered how to handle money a complete mystery. But for the first time in my life, I was able to make some sense of all this money stuff. We were not able to absorb everything, but what we could absorb was unbelievable! We could not believe what we were hearing in this class.[7]

When we reported back to our pastor about our experience, we asked if we could bring the class to our church so others could hear about this, and he said, "Sure!" I bet we taught ten or more cycles of this class at the church.

Always ask for advice—and ask as many people as you can.

You'll pick up something useful from each conversation, even if the advice isn't great. Some of it might be unhelpful, but it's still worth listening to. The truth is, a lot of people don't ask for advice for all sorts of reasons, but none of those reasons are better than actually getting the advice.

Whatever is holding you back, getting different perspectives will unlock ideas and solutions you might never come up with on your own. Don't let pride or excuses keep you from reaching out and learning from others.

> ✐ **ACTION:** Find someone today who might have something valuable to teach you about finance, business, or marriage. Also, find a consistent mentor and podcast to get life-giving advice from—and follow it!
>
> _____
>
> _____
>
> _____
>
> _____
>
> _____

13

FACING FEARS AND FINDING FREEDOM

How Growth Begins with Action

I will never forget teaching my first *Financial Peace University* (FPU) class. I was very intimidated about getting up in front of the class. I had never in my life talked in front of people. I asked my friend Matt to help out. He agreed, but little did he know I would chicken out!

When it was time for class to start, Matt got up and welcomed everyone and then said, "And now Phillip will come up here and teach the class."

That was the slowest, scariest walk I have ever done. I was able to get through it, and it was an awesome class. Thinking back, I knew the information in this class had to be shared so other people could learn what we learned. And besides, Dave Ramsey did the actual teaching by video. I was just there to help guide the discussion after the video lessons.

During the classes, I noticed that Dave mentioned several leadership and business books. As he mentioned each book, I wrote it down and ordered it the next day. Before I knew it, we had little to no workload, but I had a huge stack of books to read.

My reading skills were pretty weak, but I began to read all those books, and if the book I was reading mentioned another book, I ordered and read it too. One of the books, *The E-Myth Revisited*, mentioned a business coach. I had never heard of a business coach, but I called the number and signed up for a coach. Boy, did he have a time with me. I was about as rough a student as you could get.

One of our conversations centered around hiring someone to help with billing. I thought, *There is no way I am going to let someone mess up my billing.*

I distinctly remember one of his questions: "Are you such an ass that you think you are the only one on the planet who could do your billing correctly?"

The fact was, money was so tight that I was afraid if something was done wrong, it would sink us. However, he eventually coached me through all of that, and we hired our first office employee. What a relief this turned out to be. She actually *enjoyed* doing the job that I dreaded the mere thought of.

I found that soon after she started, my mind was free to do what I did best, which was to get more jobs for the company, make sure they were done right, and make sure the employees had plenty of direction.

Your business can only grow as much as you do.

Your business can only grow as much as you do.

I had to face one of my biggest fears—getting up in front of people during an FPU class. That was tough, but I knew I had to push through it. Then I started reading. I'll be honest—I hadn't finished a full book in my life, not even in high school. Reading was hard for me, and I was slow at it, but like anything else, the more I did it, the better I got. As I kept reading, I found myself growing, not just at work, but at home too.

I got perhaps my most important (and painful) business lesson in 2008. The lesson: Don't let your entire business become dependent on any single customer.

It was the middle of the downturn, and I was called out to meet the one site manager for Pulte Homes—my one remaining customer—that no one liked to meet with. When I got out of my truck, he began his power trip. He was the type of guy who wanted everyone to know that he was in charge. He went on and on, and I had to take it. I felt powerless and about an inch tall. He made sure of that.

✐ **ACTION:** Michael Jordan had a coach. Tiger Woods had a coach. Tom Brady had a coach. Everyone who wants to perform at a high level has a coach. So get yourself a business coach *today*.

Business Essentials, my coaching company for business owners, entrepreneurs, and leaders, offers coaching on many levels. To get a personalized coaching plan for your business, simply visit CoreBusinessEssentials .com.

_____

_____

_____

_____

_____

_____

This guy was the only one at Pulte who behaved that way.

After that meeting, I went home and told Tracy that I would never again have a customer talk to me like that. I vowed to never let a single customer be more than 10 percent of my business, so if anyone ever talked to me like that again, all they would see was the taillights of my truck.

This created an instant problem. We were in the middle of the Great Recession in the home construction business, and Pulte was my *only* customer. Forget 10 percent; they were literally 100 percent of my business!

But the fire of that conversation just kept burning inside me. It became the fuel that drove me to grow the company faster than I ever could have imagined. If I wanted them to represent only 10 percent of my business, and if they yielded roughly $200,000 per year of revenue, then I knew I had a monumental task ahead of me.

The situation fueled me for years to come. Years later, in 2018, I would have another person—someone with Pulte's competitor, Lennar Homes—try to use that same awful tactic with me. That time, however, it had a very different outcome, but I will share that in another chapter.

✐ **ACTION:** Never let any one customer be more than 10 percent of your revenue, no matter how big they are. Many $1 billion businesses have closed their doors. Also, if your customer declares bankruptcy, you are out of luck. Begin today to analyze your customers by percentage of revenue and make plans to keep them under 10 percent!

_____

_____

_____

_____

_____

14

FROM SMALL BALL TO BIG LEAGUES

Discovering New Opportunities in a Recession

We were right in the middle of the Great Recession. I wasn't worried about growth. I wasn't thinking about revenue or numbers. We were just trying to survive.

Deep in the recession, our revenue looked like this:

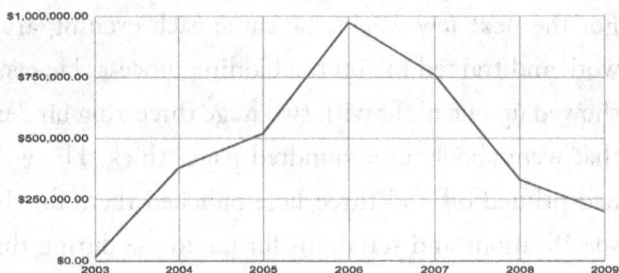

To this point, we were installing silt fences only around residential houses under construction. We were definitely playing small ball, but I had been so busy that I did not stop to see that, in addition to the residential work, there was a much bigger field that we could play on.

That year, a friend from church, for whom I will always be grateful, asked me if I knew how to estimate commercial erosion control work. He worked in the land development industry as part of the project estimating team, gathering bids from third-tier subcontractors to help his company competitively secure projects. For example, when a Walmart or a shopping center is built, all of the erosion control (silt fence) is bid out a certain way to a few contractors. By focusing only on residential erosion control, we were stuck doing the small work, but this was a chance at the big work.

I answered honestly and told him I had no idea how the process worked or how to even get started with it.

He asked if he could come over to show me how. For the next few weeks, he came each evening after work and trained me on the bidding process. He even showed up one night with two huge three-ring binders that were about three hundred pages thick. His wife had printed off and three-hole punched them for the specifications and standards for me to use during this estimating process.

I typed up my first-ever estimate and sent it over to the head estimator to hopefully win my first commercial job. The next day, I received a reply from the chief estimator. It started: "Dear sir, I can't tell you how many problems I see with your estimate. I have never seen an estimate this bad, and I cannot use it." He then went on to list everything that was wrong or incorrectly ordered on my estimate.

I was devastated to say the least. I thought, *Man, he could have just deleted it and saved me a little embarrassment here.*

Instead, I tried to focus on the opportunity in front of me. Here was a professional who could tell me exactly what I needed to do to break into this market. I saddled back up in front of my computer and replied, "Dear sir, I apologize for any inconvenience. I realize that you are a busy man in your position. If there are any pointers you could give me, it would be greatly appreciated."

He replied and graciously offered some tips, so I took him doughnuts the next day. He spent probably fifteen hours over the next couple of weeks teaching me what he needed and looked for in the estimating process. Within a few months, we picked up our first job with his company! We were contracted to put up fences around trees to protect them from being torn down on a project for the City of Charlotte.

The key to winning this job was our application and approval for a certification called SBE, which stands for *small business enterprise*. The beauty of this certification is that when the city or state awards projects to general contractors, one of the qualifications for the general contractor is that they have to award 10 to 15 percent of the project to certified small businesses on each project. That way, big businesses can't just monopolize all the projects.

Over the next few years, we really dominated the city work because we priced it very competitively, but more than that, we showed up on time every time. We were not profitable on many (if any) of these jobs, but there was a huge payoff I didn't realize at the time. Installing silt fences along the roadways made us look like the biggest game in town, because our fence had our company name printed on it every ten feet. No one wanted these jobs because they were so unprofitable, but it made us look like a titan because every road in Charlotte, it seemed, had our fence on it.

I first noticed that this strategy had started building brand recognition when friends would text me pictures of the fence somewhere and say, "Man, I see your fence everywhere." They would go on to say they went to get a haircut or went to the mall or were leaving to go out of town, or whatever they were doing, and they would see the fence.

What was so surprising was that our friends, who were not even in the construction industry, were noticing the fences. This gave me an idea—what if I started trying to get other small jobs?

So I started placing a bid on every small project from a Walgreens under construction to a McDonald's to a coffee shop. I noticed that all of these were in very high traffic flows that continued to build our brand. Even though the jobs themselves were not very profitable, they got us eyeballs and attention, which in turn gave us credibility.

Eventually, each time I approached a potential customer to work on their projects, they had already seen our work all over town, so it became pretty easy to win projects at this point. Again, we did not profit on every project—maybe not even half of them—but it gave us the reputation to get the big jobs that *were* profitable. We became a favorite of the inspectors. If an inspector noticed our fences on the job, they knew they didn't have to bother doing a thorough inspection because they knew it would be installed right and on time.

• • • • •

Be strategic in the projects you take on. Every job doesn't have to be profitable, but it must at least have a purpose. Getting recognition in strategic locations is a good purpose for this—but you should still strive to make it profitable.

Be strategic in the projects you take on.

> ✎ **ACTION:** Write three new things you can do to gain visibility. They do not have to all be profitable. Ice cream stores give free samples. Retail stores promote sales events. What three things can get you more visibility?
>
> _____
>
> _____
>
> _____
>
> _____
>
> _____
>
> _____

While all of this seemed great from the outside, it was rough on the inside of the company. The unprofitable jobs were taking their toll since money was incredibly tight.

We were not able to pay our suppliers as quickly as we liked or even according to their terms. The suppliers never hounded me for payments; I think mostly because they believed in us. They did have to reach out on occasion, but I think they also knew I would sell my house to pay my bills if I had to.

I do not believe in sticking someone with the bill. If I use something, I intend to pay for it, even if it causes me discomfort. We had a really good relationship with our two main suppliers, and I stayed in close contact, especially when my terms got stretched.

They also knew Tracy and I lived extremely frugally. No new cars, no fancy houses or gold chains. We remained who we were, and I can't help but think this also gave the suppliers confidence in us and our credit worthiness.

At this point, our revenue was more than $3 million per year, but we had never increased our pay. We kept our pay and living expenses the same from the beginning of the business. So many people raise their standard of living and consume what they are earning to the point that they can't sustain incredible growth.

As the months went by, the housing market began to slowly crawl out of the slump. We targeted homebuilders as they started to come back to life after the Great Recession. The interesting thing was, the homebuilders didn't have a silt fence guy because all the others had gone out of business. It was basically just us and XYZ Erosion Control Services (not their real name), which was the grandfather of erosion control in the Carolinas. They started out in the 1980s before all the regulations. They had more than one hundred employees. We had only ten employees, growing our workforce once again after the recession. They were an untouchable company with an incredible reputation.

✎ **ACTION:** Give your vendors and suppliers attention this week. Whether times are good or not, stay in contact with them no matter the situation.

_____

_____

_____

_____

_____

Something that did not occur to me until later was the efficiency of working for the homebuilders. My friends had small businesses too, but they worked for homeowners, so they had to earn every single customer either through advertising or word of mouth.

What I had finally figured out was most of these homebuilders were publicly traded companies or at least bigger companies. They had to sell houses to stay in business, which meant that they had entire teams just for sales. I could sell my services just one time to the builder, but they had to go out and sell their houses every day. My one sale resulted in thousands of sales every year for each builder that I worked for. Their sales team was my sales team!

This was a huge lesson for me: Don't go for one sale in a sales situation—go for something that constantly reproduces without additional effort.

Be ready. Watch for new customers and opportunities. As the economy moves—and it always will—be ready. Don't go for a single sale. Go for the relationships that bring compounding sales that multiply without extra effort.

📝 **ACTION:** List three to five ways to automate your sales system. For me, it was selling to organizations that had to employ sales teams for their own existence. If you are a service-based business, what is the equivalent of that for you? If you are a product-based business, what marketing tools would provide this for you?

_____

_____

_____

_____

15

LOCATION, LOCATION, LOCATION

How a Problem Property Became a Strategic Asset

Y ou have to move your trucks out of here by June."
I did not know how to handle this statement at the time. We had been allowed to park our trucks and store our materials for free on the construction site for several years. We worked for the national home-builder Pulte Homes, who focused on creating and building massive communities for the retirement-aged crowd. These communities were thousands of acres in size and took five to eight years to build and complete.

The beauty in this was that they had made areas available for subcontractors like me to safely store all our trucks, equipment, machines, and materials. We had an entire area just for us, so all our employees met on the site daily, which meant we didn't have the over-head expense of having an office.

Then, in June 2011, a word came that I was not prepared for. The last area to develop in this partic-ular community was where our company was located. So we had to leave and find somewhere else to base our business. But we had nowhere to go. We were just trying to survive the Great Recession, and money was tight to say the least.

As the guys worked, I started searching for a new place to relocate our business. By this time, we were working for several homebuilders again, so we needed a location convenient to all our current and future cus-tomers. A landscaper friend of mine found a place that could fit us both, but it was only temporary. We could stay there a few months. I started searching again and finally found a place for sale.

When I turned into the driveway, I could not see the house. The driveway was lined with pine trees on both sides. I slowly crept forward and then came upon a vacant two-thousand-square-foot house. I immedi-ately called the number on the sign—only to find out it was a foreclosure with lots of problems.

It was even more difficult than that. It was actually two pieces of property, and the house was sitting on both pieces. The banker on the other end of the phone let out a sigh and said that the house had not been permitted and that the previous owner had broken a lot of rules and codes.

I asked, "How much for the house?" and her reply was that they couldn't sell the house because it was on both pieces of property. Interestingly enough, only about the back right corner of the house was sitting on the adjacent property. I then asked her if she would sell me the smaller portion and a sliver of the next property to make the house sit on just the one property. Her response?

"It is against our bylaws to do anything with property lines on properties."

I said, "But you see the problem and you could fix it internally and finally sell these properties."

Her reply again: "It is against our bylaws."

I said, "Okay, can I buy the small property with most of the house on it?"

She said, "Yes, but you can only use cash. We will not allow financing."

"How much?"

"Eighty thousand."

"I will give you $62,000."

"Let me check with my higher-ups."

After a couple of days, the word came back. "Yes, $62,000."

I then said, "Can I come back and purchase a quarter of an acre from you off the big parcel for

$12,000 so that I can join it to mine and make this house whole?"

"I have to ask my supervisor."

A short while later, the answer came back in my favor: "Yes, you can, but you have to pay to draw it up."

Great!

Just one problem, though: I didn't have $62,000. I immediately listed my boat for sale, which sold very quickly, and I went to visit my grandparents. After explaining the situation, they loaned me the other $30,000 at the current interest rate because that was better than what they were getting with a certificate of deposit. I reached out to the bank and purchased my new three-acre lot with most of a house. When I went into the back corner of the house, was I trespassing? Who knows! I immediately paid someone to draw up the new plot and closed on the other quarter of an acre.

Now I had a whole property for $74,000—with a two-thousand-square-foot office and parking!

The lesson: When it comes to office space, don't pay retail or go for the nice, big facility. The facility does not make money; it is only a liability. So many people go for nicer facilities because they get excited, but it only turns into a cash drain. Since we had an incredibly small payment on this place, I was able to invest in assets that grew revenue—more trucks, equipment, and team members—without the burden of a large debt of a facility. Plus, it made for great stories.

*The lesson: When it comes to
office space, don't pay retail or
go for the nice, big facility.*

✐ **ACTION:** Shop around! It does not have to be perfect. Rent or buy the least expensive thing you can. If you have not done that, begin to make that adjustment today. There is no shame in downsizing frills to upsize profits.

_____

_____

_____

_____

_____

_____

It wasn't even a few months before code enforcement showed up to issue a violation for running a business out of a property that was zoned residential. After his visit, I had to apply and get the property rezoned from residential to commercial, which ended up being pretty easy. Now we had a three-acre commercial property for $74,000!

One thing I had not planned on was maintaining the property. There were three acres, and they were getting out of hand. At the time, construction was beginning to boom again, and we were too exhausted after rolling in at seven or eight each evening to cut the grass.

One weekend, I got an idea. Goats! Tracy and I found a couple of goats on Craigslist and brought them to the property to take care of business. They ended up being pets and never did eat any of that grass. Instead, they would both jump up on top of my Toyota 4Runner and eat the tree that I parked under. They were not doing their job, but man, they were entertaining!

After the fame of the goats, we also bought a couple of chickens to keep at the office. This was short-lived because the chickens liked to explore. One day, one of the crews came back from a jobsite laughing and told me the story.

Earlier that day, they arrived on the site to install a fence. When one of them reached into the toolbox to get his hammer, out popped a chicken, and it ran down the street of a really nice neighborhood. They spent most of the morning chasing that chicken instead of installing fences! I am so glad we didn't get in trouble for this from the homebuilder.

After this, I sold the chickens to a couple of employees. I'm told they made a pretty good soup.

16

PAYING THE PRICE FOR GROWTH

How Sacrificing Comfort Led to Success

By 2012, we had twenty employees and four trucks complete with trailers and walk-behind trenching machines. As the commercial side continued to grow, we were under increasing pressure from the customers to begin hydroseeding as one of our services or risk losing potential projects to the competitors that had this capability. This was a large undertaking because, for one, I had never used a hydroseeder.

It is basically a large dump truck, but instead of a dump bed, it has a huge tank with a blender inside it. You would fill the tank with water and add grass seed, fertilizer, and lime. The truck would then mix all the ingredients and had a huge cannon that would shoot the mixture out onto the desired area where grass was needed. This method created an environment where the grass seed had everything it needed to begin immediate germination.

We bought what we would soon name "Frankenstein": a hydroseeder that someone had pieced together with a number of parts from random machines and sold to us. Not even a year passed before we let Frankenstein retire and had to buy a better hydroseeder.

• • • • •

When you have proven the concept of your business, it is time to grow. I went to my potential customers and asked them how I could "win" bigger projects, and they told me. I then had to decide if I was willing to invest in that new opportunity. If you have proven your concept and have a good foundation, go for it! What is your next step that will propel you into the big leagues? Mine was a hydroseeder.

> ✎ **ACTION:** What is one move that could propel you into the big leagues? In what area might you be allowing doubt to hold you back?
>
> _____
>
> _____
>
> _____
>
> _____
>
> _____

Through 2011 and 2012, money was tight. Too tight. Our business and reputation were growing, but we were not making any profits. We finally came to a point where money was so low that we had to consider selling our house.

We had lived in this lake house and had the time of our lives from 2006 to 2012, but now we had to make a decision. The business was sucking cash because every time we added a person to the payroll, we had to pay them for roughly three months before we received the first check from their production. This, coupled with the fact that the bigger commercial jobs took 90–120 days to pay and the general contractor held back 10 percent of the cost for an entire year, made the situation even worse. Holding back 10 percent of a project's revenue is standard in commercial construction. This practice, known as *retainage*, is intended to ensure that contractors honor their warranty obligations and return to complete any remaining work.

As we added new commercial projects almost weekly, our need for supplies, materials, trucks, machinery, and, of course, more people to do the work grew rapidly.

This brought our budget to its knees. We had to either scale back the business or sell our house. Tracy and I talked this over quite a bit. The fact was, we had no more cash to grow with, so if we didn't take massive action to free up cash, then our growth would stall. Borrowing money—which adds risk and pressure— was not an option. Running a business while raising two toddlers and a teenager brought plenty of pressure without adding a bank breathing down my neck. I watched so many friends take on debt, only to see it backfire. When their plans didn't work out, they weren't just dealing with lost revenue; they were also stuck with loan payments that didn't go away. It seems to me that when financing is an option—when there's an "easy button"—it can make people overlook the risks in the near term. But what's often forgotten is that even if the venture succeeds, part of that new profit still has to go toward servicing the debt. Over the years, I've seen this sink people more times than I can count.

After a lot of prayer, we decided to go all in on the business. We sold our house and downsized into a much smaller home in a much less desirable area. We bounced around to a couple of smaller houses, but it was well worth it because the money we saved fueled the company—and the growth was on! We still miss that lake house today. It had 150 feet of lake frontage, a dock, and the best sunset over two different towns, all from our back porch.

Life will give you what you are willing to settle for. I had to choose whether to continue my current standard of living (on the lake) but have a mediocre-size business because of cash restraints, or whether to lower my standard of living to free up cash for a business that would bring even more cash later. There was a third option of adding loads of business debt, but adding the stress of large loans was not how we wanted to live.

> *Life will give you what you are willing to settle for.*

We chose to downgrade our life, and we really missed living on the lake, but it paid off huge. With that one transaction, we suddenly had the cash flow to grow, doubling the business three years in a row. And we were back on the lake in three years.

> ✎ **ACTION:** Is your current standard of living impeding your personal and business growth? List three ways your standard of living is holding back your true capabilities. Are you willing to settle for never knowing what could happen if you adjusted your standard of living to see what God could do with you?
>
> _____
>
> _____
>
> _____
>
> _____
>
> _____
>
> _____

17

THE BENCH IS EVERYTHING
Building a Team That Wins

In 2014, I hired our first estimator, and I also hired a person who would take over the bookkeeping. She turned out to be one of the best hires I ever made. She was consistent, caring, and hilarious. In a short time, she knew what clerical mistakes I was going to make before I even made them. She never once used it as leverage either. What an awesome person.

Another key hire that I made was probably the best of all—a hiring manager. It was the position that allowed the biggest business change and separated us from the competition and our peers more than any other move I ever made.

The workforce is still the most unsolved problem of small and medium businesses today. I realized that we succeeded or failed not due to workload or lack of sales but due to team members. If we had weak team members or not enough team members, or if we could not supply our growth due to a lack of workforce, then we were limited at best—and completely stalled at worst.

We were about twenty team members strong when I finally brought in a hiring manager. Their job was to sift through applications and find people to hire. The system was set up so they would constantly interview people for any open positions. The rule was to interview at least four people every single day. Some days, they did not achieve this, but it was the goal. Because of our growth trajectory, we needed to add roughly three to five people a month during the busy months. And finding the right fit was tough. It would sometimes take interviewing ten or more people to find one suitable person.

After all the positions were filled, they were to continue interviewing people to build a strong bench so that as soon as a team member left, we had four or five people to immediately call whom we had already interviewed and approved for hire.

We made no knee-jerk responses to applicants, and we only kept the best of the best. Also, if we had an underperforming team member who would not do what it took to win, we had a list of *A* players at our fingertips.

In every sport, the bench matters. Having fresh legs and fresh perspectives just waiting to be plugged in will lead to the success of every team. Don't react off the cuff in a staff crisis; create a bench.

• • • • •

Hire people who challenge you. Hire people who don't necessarily agree with you on everything. One of our keys to success was that I purposely hired people who thought differently than I did. We didn't need a ton of Phillips running around. We already had one of those. I wanted people who would help sharpen and strengthen the company. I took inventory of my strengths, which then enabled me to hire for my weaknesses. So many people make the mistake of hiring minions and yes-men, but that ends up completely limiting them.

Hire people who challenge you.

The year 2014 was also the year of my inventions. The reason there were not many competitors in the silt fence space was that it was such a physically demanding job.

The trencher made digging a trench exponentially easier, but after that, it was all hard manual labor. After the trench was excavated, we had to drive the four-foot-tall metal posts into the earth approximately one

NO COLLEGE, NO PROBLEM

foot deep. The posts were spaced out in a line about six feet apart, and they had to be driven into the ground with a hammer.

> ✐ **ACTION:** Begin building your bench today. Have at minimum two people (or a number equal to 5 percent of your total employees) who are ready to come on board at any given time. You will lose a certain amount to attrition, so having some people ready to go will save you time and trouble.
>
> _____
>
> _____
>
> _____
>
> _____
>
> _____

It would wear a person out quickly, as most posts needed to be struck with the hammer twenty to fifty times depending on how hard the ground was. If we installed a mile of fence, then we would need *880* posts spaced six feet apart. This was incredibly taxing on the guys.

One day, I was wondering how to make this job easier on the crews. There have been machines designed to drive posts in the ground before, but they would wear out after a week of wear and tear. They were just not tough enough for this job. One day, I saw someone using a hydraulic jackhammer to break apart concrete. As I watched him, I thought, *There is no way we could wear out one of those.*

I immediately bought one and had extra-long hydraulic hoses made to be able to reach the trencher that we already had. Then I had our mechanic weld a frame to suspend the jackhammer—and voila! We could now use our new hydraulic hammer to drive the posts into the ground. Though it was too big for our homebuilding sites, they were fabulous for the big projects.

We outfitted all our commercial crews with these hydraulic hammers, and the crews became untouchable. We were the only company with these tools. This was an incredible advantage over our competitors. As of the day that I sold the company, no one had copied it.

I had finally learned to slow the game down and identify better ways and methods. I learned that I had to be willing to call my baby ugly and that processes needed constant modification and improvement due to our growth trajectory. Always remember, what got you *here* won't get you *there*!

I also learned that running a $2 million business takes a completely different type of leader than a $1 million business. The same is true for a $2 million business going to $5 million. The business can only sustainably grow at the rate that the leader grows, and that required me to become an entirely different person.

> ✎ **ACTION:** Always evaluate your systems and processes. Begin *today*. Evaluate sales, products/services, methods, and logistics. If you are unsure how, ask someone for help. If you don't know where to start, feel free to reach out to us!
>
> _____
>
> _____
>
> _____
>
> _____
>
> _____
>
> _____

I told a friend from church, who was a mechanical engineer, about this new hydraulic hammer, and he wanted to see it in action. He visited me and was really excited. He filmed all day and took notes. I asked him if he could help me build more of the hammers because I was busy doing all I could with our growth rate. He said he thought that would be easy.

I did not hear from him for a couple of weeks, but then he reached out and invited me to lunch. At lunch, he showed me a few drawings. And then it happened. I had heard of it happening before but never directly. My friend showed me the drawing of my hammer and then showed me a new drawing where he had tweaked a few things.

And then he said: "I have made a few changes to your machine. I am going to patent it and start selling them."

I could not believe my ears. Here we were sitting and talking, friend to friend, and he was telling me that he had made enough modifications to rip off my design. I was in shock. He already had a dozen or so patents in his name from being an engineer at 3M, and he was doing this.

I told him that was a crooked thing to do, but I knew I had no legal recourse because I willingly showed it to him, and I had never attained a patent or had him sign a nondisclosure agreement. This is when I learned a lesson. People tend to develop short memories of whose idea something was when money is involved.

We have since resolved this and put it to bed, and I still consider him a friend. The lesson I learned was to make sure to have a crystal-clear understanding when dealing with someone about business intellectual property.

18

SLAYING THE MONSTER

A More Equipped, Wiser You
Can Slay Any Monster

Things were moving fast, but I still did not have any cash, and after ten years in business, we were making hardly any profits at all. However, we were slowly watching the competitors fall away.

Beginning in 2013, we added an additional $1 million-plus in revenue every single year with one exception, but as 2018 rolled around, we dropped by almost $1 million because I wanted to slow things down and clean up our systems now that we had assembled an amazing team complete with a CFO.

I would start work around 6:00 a.m., work straight through until 7:00 p.m., and then go home and crash—Monday through Saturday. By Sunday, I was exhausted, completely used up, with no margin at all. I would go to church and not hear a thing that was spoken. I would walk into the church as fast as I could, dodging anyone who looked like they might want to talk to me, and then slip out as soon as it was over. Then I would lie on the couch for the rest of the day until bedtime.

This was not how I wanted to live. It seemed to be a never-ending loop. I felt like I had created and built a monster that I had to slay each day. I needed to figure something out, but there was not enough time or energy left to come up with a solution, so I kept on doing what I was doing.

I had not put processes in place to protect myself, and my family and I suffered as a result. I was not addicted to work, but I just could not seem to get ahead no matter how fast or how hard I worked.

> ✍ **ACTION:** Make sure to put measures in place that can refill your tank. Take some time this weekend to plan how you will recharge and when.
>
> _____
>
> _____
>
> _____
>
> _____
>
> _____

Our first expansion to a new town was in Charleston, South Carolina, in 2016. We were able to get a decent amount of work on the books. However, the weather was not in our favor. It seemed to rain every other day there that year.

Erosion control work comes to a halt in the rain because of the slippery conditions. We also got the first snow in almost a decade, and it hung around for a week—or so it felt like. Plus, since we were the new guy in town, the only jobs we were awarded were the swamp jobs.

I remember one photo that the field guys sent me of a bulldozer and a massive tree machine with eight-foot-tall tires completely submerged in the mud, with only the top of the cab sticking out. No work could be done. We were not profitable, and we had to call it quits in less than a year.

One day in the spring of 2016, I was listening to the *Dave Ramsey Show* online while working in the office, and they mentioned their business brand, EntreLeadership. I did not know what this was, but I checked it out. I started listening to the *EntreLeadership* podcast online and signed up to their website so I could hear from them when I had time instead of trying to catch the show live.

One day, I got a call from Earl with EntreLeadership. Apparently, he saw that I was a subscriber to their web platform and called me. He wanted to let me know about a conference they were going to do. I think that it was the third conference they ever did.

I remember where I was standing—on the side porch at work—when he told me the details. When he mentioned the ticket price, I said he was way out of my league because I had never heard of a price like that. It was several thousand dollars for one ticket! Who had thousands of dollars for an event? I thanked him for his time and went back to work.

The funny thing is, after a few days of slaying the monster, I realized I had to do something different if I wanted something different for my family and me— and for the monster I had created.

Dave Ramsey's voice echoed in my head: "If you keep doing what you've been doing, you'll keep getting what you've been getting." I needed to learn how to run my business more effectively. I did not know how to run my business differently, and I needed a new perspective. If I did not take action or get on another path, I was destined to keep living this way. I had been exposed to people who had aged quite a bit by continuing in their business and trying to push through but never making any gains, and that was not what I wanted.

So I called Earl back. I explained to him that I had a hard time paying attention. I get distracted very easily, and sitting through an in-person event sounded difficult. That was really on my mind, but

Earl had a solution: He could make sure I was seated on the front row.

I did not buy just one platinum ticket. I bought two tickets—one for me and one for my son.

• • • • •

Invest in yourself and your education. If you grow, your business will grow too. If your business is not growing sustainably, it is because of the cold, hard fact that you haven't grown first. When you grow yourself, you are effectively working *on* the business instead of *in* the business. When you do this and hear from and speak with people who have already been where you are going, it makes a world of difference. Also, if you can, take a loved one with you. It will pay dividends their whole life!

Invest in yourself and your education. If you grow, your business will grow too.

This is where my business success came from—from growing myself, not from a booming economy. The economy was booming for everyone, just as it rains on everyone. We all know people who didn't grow or didn't grow sustainably in the booming economy. Every bit of your personal growth will benefit your family and relationships just as much as your business.

NO COLLEGE, NO PROBLEM

> 🖉 **ACTION:** Book a conference, a coach, or another type of growth opportunity today. You already know the results if you don't: You'll just stay stuck in your current situation. Book something today!
>
> _____
>
> _____
>
> _____
>
> _____
>
> _____
>
> _____

My son, Phil, worked for the business during the summers and winters while he was in high school. While pursuing his business and psychology degrees in college, he worked at a restaurant and a credit union. Once he graduated from college, he wasn't quite sure what he wanted to do for work.

I proposed, "Why don't you come work with me for six months or so while you decide what you want to do?"

That is just what he did, and he was a huge addition to the team. He was not a typical owner's son in the business; he was no Tommy Boy! He taught me a lot, bringing his new perspective, and in my opinion, he had to also unlearn a lot that the business professors taught him, who had never actually run a business but pushed their theories about how business worked.

Theories are nice, but the problem with that is someone has to pay for them.

Meanwhile, I had built a business without ever stepping foot in a college classroom. While Phil and others were learning theories, I was out in the field figuring out what actually worked. I didn't have a professor grading my decisions. If I got it wrong, the consequences were real. That's not to say college has no value, but I've learned that real-world experience is often the best teacher. Some lessons you just can't get from a textbook. And the biggest difference? I earned while I learned, instead of paying someone else for the lesson.

• • • • •

Always be ready to learn from the younger, fresher minds, even and especially if they are your kids. They have overheard the conversations at home. They know what bothers you the most. They even know your limitations no matter how hard you try to hide them. They also admire you!

19

HIGH PERFORMERS EQUALED LOW PERFORMANCE

Breaking Free from Toxic Team Dynamics

When we went to the EntreLeadership conference, we heard from a number of speakers. It included three days jam-packed with speakers (and parties each night). I had no idea what to expect, but what we learned was life-changing. Each speaker dropped wisdom on us that hit me like a sledgehammer.

They talked about focusing on your people and your customers. I had been focused on my product and survival. They talked about leadership and what leadership is. That was a concept that never occurred to me. I thought I was supposed to find work that needed to be done and then get employees to do the work. It never occurred to me to lead them, and I had never seen this modeled before. They also talked about vision and the future for you and your business. I had been focused on trying to get through each day. I didn't have a plan for where my company was going.

I learned so much that I lay in bed each evening staring at the ceiling. This is when I discovered that learning is hard work!

On the first day at the event, a man I did not know came and sat at the table with Phil and me. He looked at me and said, "Hey, if this first speaker is no good, come and get me and we will go do something fun instead."

I looked at Phil, and we laughed a second and said okay. Then the man got up and went onto the stage! That is how I learned who John Maxwell was and what he looked like.

After this, I was hooked on learning again. From attending this event, I realized that I wasn't the only one with all these problems. It was also clear that I had to start making changes with my team. I had hired anyone who was willing to work hard, but I had also hired people who did not have me, our customers, or our business in mind.

As I listened to EntreLeadership more, I began to realize that some of the team that I had hired only had themselves in mind. I had made the same mistake so many small businesspeople make: I had hired (and kept) team members who may have been higher performing than others but who were also incredibly self-absorbed and did not care about the company or their fellow teammates.

After attending the conference, I noticed that the other employees didn't perform at their best around these people because they were so hard to be around. I learned that a good team player will always outperform a high performer who lacks humility.

A good team player will always outperform a high performer who lacks humility.

For weeks, I wrestled with the decision of what to do about my employee problems. I was learning that the problem was not with the employees as much as it was with my allowing the employees to behave that way. I condoned their actions by keeping them. I was terrified that if I let them go, we would not be able to get the jobs done.

Boy, was I wrong.

As soon as I got the courage to establish a standard and let some of the high-performing, low-humility people go, everyone else stepped up. I discovered that as soon as the former employees' egos went away, the others finally had the space and felt the freedom to operate. We never missed a beat. In fact, I was shocked to realize the former "high-performing" employees were only doing about half of what I thought they were doing. The rest was just big talk and bragging.

We didn't slow down when I finally let these people go; we sped up. It was a really tough and scary time letting people go, but I trusted the process.

• • • • •

What happens if you put just a drop or two of sweetener in your coffee? It sweetens the whole cup, making every sip just a little bit better and more enjoyable.

What happens if someone puts a drop or two of poison in your coffee? It poisons the whole cup, spreading death and toxicity with every sip.

That's how I came to view bad team members who only looked out for themselves—just one toxic person poisons the whole organization. It can literally be the death of your company, so when you discover you've accidentally dropped some poison into your team, deal with it immediately. Everyone will thank you, and they will pick up the slack.

That first EntreLeadership event was so mindblowing and made such an immediate impact on my business that I went to several more. Sure, it was expensive, but it turned out to be the best investment I've ever made in my company. Every dollar I've spent on EntreLeadership events and material has come back to me tenfold.

☑ **ACTION:** Evaluate everyone on your team today. Are there any high performers that make it miserable for everyone else? If so, give them a week to correct and if they do not, let them go. If you look around and see a team member that you would not hire again, give them a week to correct, and if they do not, let them go. The rest of your team will thank you.

_____

_____

_____

_____

_____

_____

We had quite a bit of fun at these EntreLeadership conferences, and we attended eight in a row. They really went all out, and there was always a huge opening ceremony. During one of the conferences, they rented out the Dallas Cowboys' football stadium for the opening, which was really cool. They had it all decked out. There was an area set up where we could kick footballs through the field goal, and they had an area for practicing passing skills. Of course, there was also food, drinks, and music.

One night of that Dallas trip, our leadership team rented scooters and had a blast ripping up the town like Hells Angels on scooters. We laughed and played chase on those things for hours. We jumped sidewalks. We rode mechanical bulls in the bars. There was no talk of work, just full-grown adults tearing up the town like kids!

• • • • •

Don't take yourself too seriously. Have fun! What is the purpose of all you are doing if you can't enjoy it along the way? The laughter and fun will give you the energy you need to get to where you want to go.

20

THE $13 MILLION GAP
Rising to the Challenge

Boom—I didn't see this next event coming.

In 2017 I received a phone call that would change the game for us . . . again. We had been bringing the heat even more than I knew.

We had started out in our business doing anything we could to gain momentum. Then we pivoted to primarily installing silt fencing on house lots. After a while, we started going after commercial projects too. Of course, we only ever got the small commercial projects, and that was due to one reason and one reason only: The granddaddy of all erosion control companies in the Carolinas, XYZ Erosion Control (not their real name), had all the big, juicy work.

They had been around since the 1980s, and the original founder gave the business to one of his employees, Gregory (again, not his real name), in the late 1990s.

Gregory brought on a couple of his relatives as partial owners and divided up their crews between the three of them. They had an awesome reputation and did fantastic work. They would work fourteen-hour days, six days a week. This was impressive to everyone, but no one predicted what would happen next.

Tracy and I bought a house in 2015 in a neighborhood for which XYZ performed the erosion control. Occasionally, I would see Gregory working in our neighborhood, and I would go outside and chat with him. He was an extremely likable and genuine guy. I was really impressed with him because he ran this one-hundred-plus-person operation in his twenties.

We talked about different customers, and he talked about how many hours they were working. He said that after fourteen hours, he then had to do the billing for the work. He asked me how we were doing, and I told him we were busy but were not doing the caliber of jobs he was doing. We had great conversations; I always enjoyed talking with him.

One day, Gregory called me with a downcast voice. They had suffered a tragedy on the jobsite and lost one of their employees. He asked if I would finish that particular job for him because his employees could not bear to go back to that site after witnessing the event. I offered my condolences and thanked him for trusting us to help out. I was very proud that I had operated in a manner that he felt comfortable asking me for this.

· · · · ·

Always try to have good relationships with the competition when possible, and always be there for others—including your competition. At the end of the day, we are all people working to feed our families and build a financially secure situation for ourselves. Competition is healthy and usually helps create better products at better costs, but it can get out of hand, and we forget that everyone is human. If you are impressed with your competitor, tell them. They might need to hear it that day!

Always try to have good relationships with the competition when possible, and always be there for others—including your competition.

In late 2017, I received a phone call from Gregory while Tracy and I were on our way to visit a customer. As he started to talk, and as I slowly realized what he was saying, I pulled over to the side of the road to finish the call.

Gregory was tired of missing his family. He was tired of the long days. The loss of his employee's life the previous year was weighing heavily on him, and he didn't want the responsibility of that anymore. He told me he was selling his business to his largest customer.

Here was the kicker: XYZ was not going to compete with me anymore.

His largest customer, ABC Grading Company (name also changed), desperately needed employees and machines because they were taking market share hand over fist from their competitors, so they were going to train the XYZ employees to do mass grading.

As soon as we hung up, I said to Tracy, "This leaves a $13 million hole in the Charlotte market." I was in shock. I couldn't believe it. This was incredible. We were ready to grow!

Over the next six months, we landed a decent amount of their previous customers, but so did our other small competitors. This became a true blessing for us because at the end of the day, we could not have taken on all $13 million of XYZ's previous work at one time; we would have failed too.

However, some of the small guys got greedy and tried to take on too much work. That was fine with me, because it gave us time to grow slowly and purposely as we digested the smaller portion we took on. The other businesses who took on too much slowly but surely failed due to the size of the jobs and created a bad name for themselves in the process. So when their customers became dissatisfied with their performance, we were right there—willing and ready to work.

We were growing faster than I could have ever dreamed, and even better than that, we were getting larger and more desirable jobs. The growth was tough, so I decided to phone a friend.

FROM SURVIVING TO THRIVING

The CFO That Boosted Our Profits

I n 2018, I reached out to Mike, a guy who had a successful landscaping company he had started around the same time I started my company. I called him to ask for his advice about some of the growing pains I was struggling with.

As we spoke, Mike said, "You need to meet my two friends named Gary."

The next day, I called both Garys. "Gary One," as the contact said and still says in my phone, was his business coach. "Gary Two" was his chief financial officer (CFO). I didn't even know what a CFO was.

Gary Two began to explain to me the role of a CFO, but then he told me that he couldn't help me because he was so busy. He instead introduced me to

155

another guy he thought could help us part time (fractionally), but they turned out not to be a good fit for us.

However, Gary One introduced me to his friend, another CFO looking for a place to land. By this time, we were a little over $8 million in revenue and still not making much more than a paycheck at best. We were flowing through lots of money but keeping almost none of it. I knew after the CFO told me what he needed for a salary that there was no way I could afford something like that.

But then he said, "What *can* you afford?"

So either he was desperate or God was providing this and I had to decide. I made the only offer I thought I could afford, and for a trial period, he accepted.

I could not believe the changes and improvements that he made during and after his trial period. Through new processes, ideas, and budgeting, he managed to improve our profitability from 5 percent to 20 percent, which really began to free up cash flow. The next year, we grew 50 percent and were even more profitable.

Some of the other skills our CFO had were analysis of the data and negotiation. He helped us realize that we needed to increase the price for one of our core customers as we had not raised our prices since we started for them four years earlier.

We had a meeting with this customer at a big conference table in their corporate office, and the customer told us how important they were in the market and that losing their business over a price increase would be a shame.

They then asked, "What percentage of your work are we? Are we not the majority of your business?"

Armed with info from my CFO, I said, "No, sir. You are 10 percent of our customer base. It would hurt, but we could replace it with a little work."

My CFO then went on to make a full presentation, including current market data, our rising costs due to inflation, and their profitability as our customer as compared to our other customers. The data showed that we were actually better off terminating them as a customer than keeping the current pricing. We were the only company in town that could handle their workload.

We got the cost increase that day!

• • • • •

Don't hire for who and what you need today. If your plan is strong growth, you need to hire people who are capable of running a company twice your current size so you don't outpace your talent. Early on, I hired for who I needed at the moment. This regularly presented problems because we were adding an additional $1 million per year, and we very quickly outpaced their capabilities.

I wondered how my star players suddenly became underperformers. It baffled me. It took me a long time to figure out what was happening. Then I figured it out: It was due to our growth trajectory. The people who were rock stars when we were at one level couldn't keep up when the business moved to the next level. But after hiring such an awesome CFO and bookkeeper/controller, along with my son and a few other key hires, we had lots of room to grow because they were all more than capable of where we were—and more importantly, they were all willing to grow themselves.

More importantly, they were all willing to grow themselves.

✐ **ACTION:** Set goals, then hire your leadership team based on where you are going, not where you are today. Make sure your team members have margin to grow with you.

_____

_____

_____

_____

_____

Early in 2018, I was approached by an erosion control contractor out of Atlanta, Georgia. They made me an offer for our company. He told us that if we didn't accept the offer, his company would come to Charlotte to take the work.

Tracy, my son, and I looked over the numbers. After the dust settled, we would pocket a little over a million bucks. It seemed like a lot of money, but we were not at peace with it. We called and talked with some friends, and eventually, I called Gary One for advice. He told me after a couple of hours of talking that I would regret selling, because I really enjoyed my team and leading into the unknown.

He was right. I loved every win. I loved hitting new heights with the team. I loved the camaraderie and the fun at the office. Then he said, "I don't want to coach you until you decide if you want to keep the company." So we decided to keep the company and take on the challenge. This company that I had just turned down was more than six times our size with way more money than we had. We were a little intimidated, but we also loved a good challenge.

They never gained any market share from us, although they did take market share from our competitors. They used the cheap model using unskilled workers and undercutting everyone by more than 30 percent. We used fast, high-horsepower workers.

We charged a higher price, but we could get the projects finished on or before the deadline—and with an excellent product. We actually considered cutting our price to match theirs, but we would have had to give up quality or speed, which was completely off the table. It turned out people wanted their jobs done fast and right more than cheap, slow, and low-quality.

Timing and compatibility—neither of these were in my favor on this deal. It was too little money to retire on, and at forty-three, what would I do? This was definitely not the right time to sell, and our companies' values were nowhere near compatible. If you are not at peace with a large decision like this, don't do it—whatever it is.

22

BEYOND THE JOBSITE
*Creating a Culture of
Connection and Celebration*

Your employees can be both your biggest source of joy and biggest struggle. I decided early on that we wanted our team to be home with their families in the evenings and not work eighty-hour weeks like the industry standard. I did not feel right about being home myself but expecting everyone else to work long hours. Plus, they couldn't have a successful, happy family if they were working long hours consistently. If your employees are struggling with relationships at home, you can guarantee they will not be able to focus fully on work.

Each year, we would have a summer company party at my house. The employees would bring their

NO COLLEGE, NO PROBLEM

entire families. We would swim in the pool, and I would take them out tubing behind the boat.

Imagine more than one hundred people, a mechanical bull, dunking booths, money tunnels, swimming, tubing, and incredible amounts of food. I would attach three four-person tubes behind my wake boat, and we would have twelve people on the tubes and twelve people in the boat watching. It was a lot of fun! For some of the crowd, it was their first time being on the lake. The people who didn't go out on the boat stayed back around the pool. I was so impressed and in awe that so many of the people would show up and bring their families to the party.

I actually heard some of them say that they had never been to their boss's house or even spent time with them. It was just as fun for us as it was for them. Watching so many people of all ages have fun and cut loose was indescribably fulfilling. It was so awesome to have created an environment for this to happen and watch it grow. We focused on people first, and it showed.

We focused on people first, and it showed.

We also had Christmas parties every year, and one of our employees even cooked and brought a goat. We had games and prizes for everyone.

One day, I bought a large pull-behind smoker for the company. I wanted to serve the employees more than just at Christmas and the summer party. It turned out even better than I thought it would. The field managers started volunteering to cook. Our office staff and managers would also band together and cook meals and serve the homeless at the local shelter several times a year.

We started a monthly tradition where a couple of managers would cook for the team, so when they returned from the jobsites, they had a meal to gather around and eat while they hung out together. When it was the field manager's turn to cook, he would split his schedule up among the other guys and go buy enough food for one hundred people—on the company card of course. The office staff would sometimes help prepare the food in the conference room, and he would spend the day cooking or smoking whatever he was serving that month.

The aroma of the food would drive us crazy all day. As the crews would come in from their jobs for the day, the entire office staff would go outside and start eating. We would be out there for hours, greeting everyone and playing cornhole, but mostly feeding our faces.

Some months, it was freezing, and some months it was unbelievably hot, but it was awesome to be a part of this experience. Some of the guys were exhausted and

NO COLLEGE, NO PROBLEM

made a plate to go, but most stayed back to hang out. Some of them even stayed until nine in the evening.

I was not one of those people.

• • • • •

Your team wants and needs to eat together. If you can bring your team together and laugh together, they will not be so quick to jump to the next company for a little more money. Every company needs to be about more than just increasing the bottom line. As leaders, we create an environment where people want to be and want to excel in. We were untouchable in work and in fun!

> 🖉 **ACTION:** Plan your event today. It will lower your turnover and increase morale, which increases productivity. The people crave this!
>
> _____
>
> _____
>
> _____
>
> _____
>
> _____
>
> _____

One day, I was talking to Mike, the guy who introduced me to Gary One and Gary Two, about my company's soccer games. On some Saturdays, some of our team members would meet at a soccer field for an internal soccer game. They would bring their kids, and we would eat and have a good time.

As I mentioned this to Mike, he wanted in. He said he had a number of soccer players at his company, and the trash talk immediately started. We worked for several of the same builders, so the talk got ramped up quite a bit. Then, another landscaping contractor heard about it and made a video officially throwing his hat into the ring.

We rented an indoor soccer field a month or so later—and let me tell you, it was brutal. What started out as soccer quickly became a soccer-rugby hybrid. To say it was intense is an understatement.

I didn't tell Mike that all my guys played in leagues on Sundays and had won multiple championships. What Mike didn't tell me was that his guys did too, and he actually had a semi-pro retired Charlotte Eagle on his team.

By the end of the game, there were plenty of questionable calls because of one simple detail: I hadn't thought to hire a referee, so we had to agree on calls on the fly. It was a lot of fun and got heated at times. What an experience! It was fun to bring two different construction trades together and get the town talking.

· · · · ·

Strategic relationships are gold. We did not necessarily have a financial relationship, but we worked with a lot of the same customers and had a good relationship. We regularly traded wisdom, advice, struggles, and even complaints. If I had not sought out this relationship, I would never have met my business coach, my charter pilot, my CFO, or even my amazing accounting firm. Most of all, I would not have Mike as a good friend.

✎ **ACTION:** Build a strategic partnership this week. Mike was a competitor at one point before dropping erosion control to focus on his landscaping and hardscapes. Strategic partnerships are golden! Build one new partnership every month.

_____

_____

_____

_____

_____

_____

23

HIRING THE INSIDE EDGE
Bringing On Board Expertise from the Other Side of the Table

At this point, we were adding a homebuilding customer every few weeks. It was exhilarating! Each new homebuilder came with their own sales team, and for every house they sold, we were the ones installing the erosion control measures. It was a great feeling, but there was a major downside: Every single homebuilder had their own proprietary systems—different accounting processes, purchase order systems, invoicing procedures, field verification methods, and insurance compliance requirements. Nothing was consistent from one customer to the next.

I was signing on new customers left and right, but we couldn't keep up with all their different processes for actually getting paid. The receivables were piling up, and the tension within the team and with customers was growing. We were overwhelmed by the extreme growth, and no one had the time to learn all these complex systems.

That's when I had an idea: I needed to hire someone who already knew these processes inside and out. I remembered a few project managers we worked with—employees of the homebuilders—had mentioned they were ready for a change. These were people who already understood the systems from the inside. I reached out to two of them, and after a few days of consideration, one of them gave his two weeks' notice and came aboard.

I know hiring a customer's project manager could be risky, but I handled it the right way. I spoke with his supervisor, who already knew he was looking for his next step. Everything was done on good terms, and the transition was seamless.

The beauty of this hire was that he already knew the internal systems for several of our homebuilding customers. He'd worked for a number of them, climbing the ranks over time. Like so many in that industry, he had started in an entry-level position with one homebuilder before being approached by another with a better offer. By moving up the ladder this way, he had eventually become an area project manager, gaining experience with multiple builders along the way.

When he joined our team, it was like night and day! His inside knowledge allowed him to design our purchase order system to align with our customers' processes. He also helped us understand and provide what our customers needed, things we hadn't even realized we were missing.

This turned out to be one of the best hires I ever made. In fact, over the years, there were five key hires I made in this business that completely changed the game for us, driving explosive growth and setting us apart from the competition. This was one of them.

• • • • •

When your business is experiencing rapid growth, you have to think differently. I had a choice: either keep growing while the opportunity was there or slow down to learn and implement a long list of new systems. I wasn't willing to pump the brakes. Growth at that pace isn't always available, and honestly, no one in our company was passionate about learning those systems. Instead of trying to reinvent the wheel, I decided to bring in someone who already understood the "wheel design"—something I didn't know.

> *Instead of trying to reinvent the wheel, I decided to bring in someone who already understood the "wheel design"—something I didn't know.*

Who can you hire that has the knowledge and strengths you don't have? It can feel intimidating to bring someone onto your team who knows more than you in certain areas, but if your goal is to grow as a leader and build your organization, there's no better way to do it. So what challenges are you facing right now that a key hire could solve for you?

> ✏️ **ACTION:** Make a list of the people who would know the answer to your largest problems. Don't judge the list, just write it. Could you hire any of these people? Reach out to them, and you might be surprised!
>
> _____
>
> _____
>
> _____
>
> _____

24

PERMISSION TO PAUSE: THE LEADERSHIP RESET

Rediscovering Peace Amid the Chaos

By 2018, we were in our eighth straight year of incredible growth. This sounds awesome for headlines and small talk, but it was exhausting and taking its toll. By this time, I had hired an extremely capable team, complete with a CFO and project managers. I had to learn how to build a business that was bigger than I had ever dreamed of, and on top of that, I had to learn leadership because I wanted our business not just to be transactional—I wanted it to truly embody that we were people dealing with other people.

> *I had to learn leadership because
> I wanted our business not just to
> be transactional—I wanted it to
> truly embody that we were people
> dealing with other people.*

All of this was very taxing. Our team was super capable and constantly progressing, so staying in front of them was quite a challenge. Part of my role was to make sure we were going to have enough work six to eighteen months down the road because by this point, we were approaching seventy employees.

It took quite a bit of preparation to keep the pipeline of upcoming projects and opportunities open in case a customer floundered or went out of business, which did happen from time to time. For every three employees I added, I would have to purchase an entire rig consisting of a truck, trailer, and trenching machine, which would cost roughly $120,000 per rig. Then I would have to pay that crew for roughly two months before I would receive the income for them due to the delayed pay cycle of the construction industry. This was stressful to say the least—but we continued to grow.

One evening, I stood in our dining room talking to Tracy. I was so stressed, not because of any particular situation but from the weight of everything combined. I told her that I was beside myself and just numb. I couldn't feel a thing. I couldn't enjoy anything. I couldn't breathe. I needed to be alone. I needed the noise to stop.

We had been on a vacation. We had been on some short trips, but my thoughts and phone still followed me around. Standing at the table, I told her I needed some time to myself. I needed to go walk the Appalachian Trail or something.

"Do it," she said. "Go take care of yourself. We will be fine."

I couldn't believe my ears. She gave me permission to go on a selfish vacation by myself. I then argued and told her how it was too selfish for me to do that. She insisted and told me that she needed me to be healthy. I couldn't believe it.

So I sat down at that dining room table and started looking for a place to go. I quickly decided not to go to the wilderness by myself—that seemed to be where a lot of bad news stories started—but I was finally able to land on a place. It seemed crazy, and it was the complete opposite of the wilderness, but I had no idea just how much this trip would change my life forever.

I booked it immediately. I had never in my life been anywhere by myself. Not once. The plan was to be alone and have as little stimuli or human interaction as possible.

The next day, I went to the grocery store and bought a cooler full of sandwich meats, lettuce, tomatoes, mayo, and wraps. These would be my meals for the next four days. Then I grabbed two books: *As a Man Thinketh* by James Allen and *Failing Forward* by John Maxwell. When it was time to leave, I looked at Tracy and asked her, "Are you sure you're okay with this?" I was a little intimidated and nervous but also excited.

She said, "Go. I love you. Go."

I plugged Charleston Harbor Resort into my GPS, and off I went. I didn't even research what the place looked like or exactly where it was. I didn't have the mental margin for that, so I let the GPS do the work. I don't remember much of that first drive or even checking in. All I remember is crashing onto the bed, where I would hibernate for the next four days. I did not respond to texts, answer phone calls, check out social media, or even read the news on my phone. I arrived, took a nap, then got out one of my books and laid it beside me.

I finally took a walk around the room and onto the balcony, and I could not believe the beauty of this place. It was on the harbor (duh, that was in the name of the resort, but I was so exhausted I didn't even compute that). I watched marvelous, behemoth cargo ships cruise by just outside of my balcony.

Then I got back into bed and started reading *Failing Forward* by John Maxwell. I could not read more than one page before laying the book down and thinking, *Man, I am blowing this leadership thing.* I could not believe how many things I was doing wrong in business and leadership. I was making mistakes out of sheer exhaustion and ignorance.

Before I got through the first chapter, I kept thinking, *How could these people still be working for me? I am so unqualified to run a business at $12 million in revenue with seventy team members. What am I even doing?*

That first evening, I think I read only one chapter before I went out to my truck to make a deli wrap. When I got back to the room, I switched on the TV, tuned to CNBC, and watched reruns of *Shark Tank* until I drifted off to sleep.

· · · · ·

The next morning, I woke up at five. I think this was the first morning in ten years that I had woken up alone. The only noises in the room were made by me. No distractions. No one needed anything or wanted anything. No one was asking, "What's for dinner?" or "What are we doing today?" No kids were complaining about being bored. It was just me and God—although, at the time, it felt like it was just me.

I went out on the balcony and started reading again. It was the same experience as the day before. I went back in and found some paper and a pencil and started taking notes. Before lunch, I had completely filled up the hotel notepad! I stuck the notes in my book and struck out for the store. There was no way I was going to be able to retain all of that, so I needed a notebook. As I read, I learned that failing was part of learning, and that it was okay!

I kept reading throughout the morning, then I made my lunchtime wrap, took a nap, and then repeated. I read until it was time to make my wrap for dinner, then watched *Shark Tank* until I fell asleep. By the second morning, I felt different. I felt energized. I felt rested. I felt . . . well, good!

I even called Tracy to check in. Everyone was fine. She wanted to know how I was, and for the first time in as long as I could remember, I was able to say "Good," and actually mean it.

As the fourth day rolled around and it came time to leave, I was a completely different person. I was rested and actually enjoying the things I was seeing. I found some John Maxwell YouTube videos and listened to those on the way home.

Somehow, I knew this trip would be the turning point in my life for so many reasons. I had gone on a trip by myself for the first time ever. I had achieved stillness and quietness for my soul. I had studied and learned in complete solitude, with the only interruption being looking out my window to see massive cargo ships and amazing dolphins. I had a wife who wanted me to be healthy more than she wanted me to help at home (I do wonder if I had even been much help in the state that I was in). I had a new outlook. I had a new earthly heaven. I had experienced peace.

> ✐ **ACTION:** Get away. Get quiet. Get peace. It can be unnerving in the quiet. It will feel unproductive. It might even feel like you don't need it. If so, understand that this is untrue, no matter the situation. Everyone needs some peace and quiet—perhaps more often than others depending on your situation and leadership level. We are constantly bombarded with ads, notifications, and people trying to get our attention. After all, that's how they make their money, so it benefits *them* to distract *you*. For this reason and a million others, protect yourself and prioritize making time to get away and get quiet.
>
> _____
>
> _____
>
> _____
>
> _____
>
> _____
>
> _____

25

MORE THAN WORK
The Heartbeat of a
Purpose-Driven Team

I had a new energy for my family and my work when I got back home. I was able to enjoy church. I was not annoyed if someone wanted to talk. I felt completely different!

I immediately scheduled another trip for the following month. The second trip was identical except for a few differences. I decided to walk across the enormous bridge that separated Charleston from Mount Pleasant. I put in my earbuds, listened to John Maxwell videos, and walked across the bridge, then had lunch and walked back. It was about a nine-mile round trip. This gave me plenty of exercise and time to listen to good teaching. It was incredible.

After I returned from my walk, I resumed my reading. The following day, I took my book and rode the water taxi into Charleston where I read my book while having lunch at a waterfront restaurant. This was such a surreal time. My reading was having an even greater impact on me on the second visit than on the first visit.

After this second visit, I scheduled a new visit for every other month—sometimes every month. Tracy even took my spot a couple of times to experience it for herself. Some of my visits were only for a night or two, and I could tell a huge difference in myself between going for one night versus three nights.

I later asked myself, *Why did it take me so long to take this trip?* I needed to be by myself. Even Jesus withdrew on many occasions to pray and to be by himself. Today, I don't believe that we can be who we truly are supposed to be and hear what we truly need to hear if we don't purposely and intentionally withdraw from the noise for a set period of time. No phone, no tablet, no friends, no TV, no distractions. Just our soul and God.

No phone, no tablet, no friends, no TV, no distractions. Just our soul and God.

When I returned home from my trip, I noticed something really cool. Even though I had not been functioning at 100 percent, the business had an awesome thing going. At one point we were in a regular weekly field manager meeting. This was a meeting where we met with all the field managers to get updates from the field. Midway through their updates, I stopped the meeting and said, "I want an update that has nothing to do with a fence. Please tell me something that has nothing to do with environmental things."

> ✎ **ACTION:** Get away on a regular basis. Don't let much time pass before you press pause on the pressure. Things will be much clearer for you when you return. Also, don't use this as a time for bars and socializing. Use it to be quiet, to think, and to meditate.
>
> _____
>
> _____
>
> _____
>
> _____
>
> _____
>
> _____

I had just gotten back from one of my trips, and I wanted to know that we were more than just a transactional company, that we were actual people, and that we were making a difference.

There was silence for what felt like a whole minute, which is a long time in a meeting. Then one of the guys said, "I stopped to talk to one of the project managers on-site, and she told me that her dad had just passed away." He went on to say that they talked for some time about her dad.

When he finished, another field manager piped up. "I just had an hour-long conversation with a customer about his family dog that had just died, and they were all taking it very hard."

Before I knew it, every single one of the field managers told a story that day of similar situations. That was probably the proudest I have ever been of my company. We were *not* just a transactional company. We were actual people doing work and life together, and our customers trusted us enough to tell us stuff about their lives. This and what was about to happen in 2020 were my two proudest moments in my working life.

· · · · ·

To have a durable company with an infinite game mindset, you have to offer more than just your core product or service. Most businesses are mainly about relationships. Think about it. Why do so many people go to Chick-fil-A? Everyone has chicken sandwiches, but we go because it just *feels* better there—a cleaner environment and a courteous staff. We will wait in line at Chick-fil-A when the other chicken places are next door with no one in line. Why? Because it's not *just* about the chicken, and it's not *just* about the transaction. It's about the experience and the relationship—how well Chick-fil-A takes care of us.

> ✏️ **ACTION:** Check with your team. I bet they already have stories to share about powerful team and customer interactions. Plus, they would feel empowered if the leader asked to hear about them!
>
> _____
>
> _____
>
> _____
>
> _____
>
> _____
>
> _____

26

LEARNING TOGETHER
From Conference Room
to Family Room

Over this period, I really wanted to share with my team members some of the financial and life principles I had learned over the years. So I started bringing groups of ten of my field staff into the conference room once a week, fed them lunch, and played Dave Ramsey's *Financial Peace University* videos. After the videos, we would have discussions.

The team was hyped about learning! After just the first week, I started receiving texts from them saying, "I just saved up $500!" or "I just saved up $1,000!" That may not sound like a lot to you, but it was the first time some of these people had ever had $1,000 cash sitting in the bank. Some of them didn't think they'd *ever* be able to do that, but now they were hitting that milestone and even more!

One of them texted me to let me know he had paid off his car and decided not to go into debt for a new one. They had been on the fence about getting a loan on a new car but decided not to dive right back into debt.

It was an amazing experience. I got to watch firsthand as they grew in knowledge that then moved into wisdom. More than one came up to me in private and said, "No one has ever tried to share stuff like this with us. I can't thank you enough. This will change my family forever now that I know what to do!"

We got so much good feedback from those who took our first classes that we got the Spanish-language version of the class and started offering classes for our Spanish-speaking team members. The questions they asked and the glimmers of hope and knowledge I saw from them completely filled my heart.

To this day, I still get texts and calls from my old team members who are excited to tell me they hit huge goals like paying off their house or even simpler things like avoiding a financial trap. Some have also called to tell me they finally achieved their permanent citizenship. That stuff makes my day!

By this time, I had attended around eight Entre-Leadership conferences. Each year, I would take at least four people from my leadership team with me.

I learned after the first event that when I tried to go back and teach what I had learned, I sounded like a bumbling idiot. I was learning the materials and the content well enough to make massive changes myself, but I could not articulate to others what I had learned. So I simply decided to take people with me. I could tell it was helping them at work, and they told me it was also helping them at home too. The principles are all the same. It turns out that things like servant leadership and treating people well are equally important in both places!

These conferences were not just teaching business principles; they were teaching principles to live by at home, in business, and everywhere. One of the biggest lessons I learned from these speakers and teachers was that each team member I employed had individual goals and dreams of their own.

I had never thought of this before. Most of the people didn't have anyone who wanted to hear about their goals and dreams. I realized that if I could learn to listen and play a small part in encouraging them to chase after their dreams—whether it was buying a home, going on that special trip, pursuing a needed skill, or getting out of debt—they loved and cared for the team more. I kept a record of their goals, and I would check in with them to see how they were doing. I still get texts and calls from some of them wanting to share their milestones and achievements.

. . . . .

Your team members have goals too. They might not, however, know a path to achieve them like you. You're the entrepreneur. You're wired to find a path to victory and to dare to dream big. If you learn to use your gifts and personal drive to help them achieve their own goals, they will be on fire for you! Is that manipulative? No! You're not doing it to earn their loyalty; you're doing it because you value these people.

> *If you learn to use your gifts and personal drive to help them achieve their own goals, they will be on fire for you!*

I once heard John Maxwell answer the question, "What if I invest all of this time and money into them, and they leave?"

His answer? "What if I don't invest time and money in them, and they stay?"

As I attended these conferences and feasted on the books and coaching, something was happening at home. It wasn't good, and it took me a while to figure it out.

Tracy and I were having a harder time agreeing on things. We were really struggling. She looked at me as if I were babbling when I talked. Then it occurred to me. I had been so focused on my learning and growing, but I had not taken her along for the ride. I was so consumed with winning at work, and it was so addictive, that I completely took my eye off the ball at home.

> 📝 **ACTION:** Ask your direct reports about their goals. Check in on them quarterly to check on their progress. They will thank you for remembering. There's a decent chance they don't have anyone in their corner.

_____

_____

_____

_____

_____

I immediately bought her tickets to the next upcoming conferences so we could learn together. Then I started sharing the things that I was reading and listening to with her. This made a tremendous difference!

I am not going to say we agreed on everything after this—after all, it is a marriage—but we began learning together. She was an instant hit with the people at the

NO COLLEGE, NO PROBLEM

conferences, as she is an extreme extrovert. She ended up onstage in contests and forged a lot of new relationships with the speakers and hosts.

I realized I was learning new things but wasn't sharing them at home. Just because you've learned something doesn't mean that the people around you learned it.

> ✍ **ACTION:** Include your spouse in what you are learning. They want to be included even if they don't work in the business. You can build your marriage or relationship while building your business. They do not have to be separate or at separate times. As an old African proverb states: "Remember, if you want to go fast, go alone. If you want to go far, go together!"

_____

_____

_____

_____

27

FROM CRISIS TO CAMARADERIE

A Team's True Spirit

My family and I had just arrived home from vacation in late January 2020 when things started to get weird. By March, no one knew much about what was going on, but we'd all started to hear bits and pieces. I gathered my leadership team and field managers in the front office. Everyone knew something was up, and the air was filled with suspense, as most of us had been hearing about a sickness called COVID-19. I told them to go shopping because I heard that stores were running out of supplies, and then everyone was to come back to work to discuss what was going to happen and what it would potentially look like.

The government was forcing businesses to close, making knee-jerk decisions that put them on a collision course with widespread panic. We all knew there was a good chance the government would close us down for a while. The first thing I wanted my employees to know if that happened was that, if money ran short, I would be the first to stop getting paid. I wasn't going to keep cashing my paychecks if it meant endangering any of my team members' families.

Then something amazing happened. Each member of my leadership team started volunteering the same thing.

"If needed, hold my pay to make sure everyone else gets paid," Rick, the CFO, piped up first.

One after the other, they all chimed in with, "Hold my pay if needed."

"Let the field guys get paid first," was the overwhelming response.

What a team! Who would have guessed that we had such a loving organization where people were willing to give up their paycheck to make sure the folks under them in the organization got paid.

As the pandemic spread, the opposite of what we expected happened. The work poured in. Some of the homebuilders followed the government's lead and panicked and closed down, while the more intelligent ones took advantage of the freed-up workforce. No one ever came close to missing a paycheck, but they now had my heart forever after that meeting. I had known for a while that we had something different, and this proved it.

• • • • •

The leader of an organization usually reaps the biggest reward. But that also means the leader—not the team members—should be taking the biggest risks. Today, many businesses are quick to lay people off before letting lean times affect an executive's pay. A true leader of character will take the hit and criticism first. As author Simon Sinek famously said (and even titled a book), "Leaders eat last."

> *The leader—not the team members—*
> *should be taking the biggest risks.*

> ☑ **ACTION:** In times of confusion, immediately share the plan daily with the team. Trust me, they are hearing the opposite information many times per day from social media and news outlets.

28

FLYING THROUGH GROWTH
From Miles to Minutes

Our first attempt at expanding to a new region, Charleston, in 2016 hadn't gone well. Our second attempt was much more successful.

We expanded into the Raleigh-Durham area first. In November 2019, I reached out to our current customers from Charlotte that had a national or regional presence and were able to launch in Raleigh right away. They already had companies that provided the same services that we did, but there were communities that were too far out or not convenient, so the builders asked us if we would consider the inconvenient locations. *Yes* was the immediate answer.

We took all the communities that no one else wanted to service, which meant we were really spread out and not very profitable, but at least we were in business. Since we were using a long-term mindset this time, it was easier to do.

We did not set up a location right away. We actually serviced Raleigh from our Rock Hill branch for a while to prove the concept would work. For the crew, this meant taking a three-hour trip to Raleigh, working all day in the communities, and then taking a three-hour trip back home. Those were really long days, but the guys killed it because they knew they were a part of something really cool.

Everyone was excited to see where we could go as a team. They were just as proud to expand and be a part of it as I was!

This team continued to work in the Raleigh market while we began to hire locally.

Not long after we established the Raleigh location, I wanted to connect with the team and share some of the financial principles I had learned over the years. So I took my TV off the bedroom wall, threw it and ten chairs in the back of my pickup, and hit the road. When I arrived at the Raleigh office, I set up the TV and soundbar on the tailgate of my truck and started leading new *Financial Peace University* classes with them, just as I'd done with the rest of the team. It was amazing—they had never heard this information before.

• • • • •

Always look retrospectively at a failed attempt so you don't repeat it. Also, don't bet the farm on a new idea. Test it in small increments first. It only took three years before we attempted expanding a second time, but our newly built team was more than capable by then. It was a strain—expanding will always be a strain—but it was exciting.

Three years before, I had failed, but I studied the points of failure, and we knew what to avoid. Instead of immediately getting excited and renting a facility, we did a trial where we launched each day out of our Rock Hill office or rented hotel rooms until we were able to prove the concept and gain ground.

> ✏️ **ACTION:** If you have experienced failure, invite a few friends to help you do an autopsy on the situation to find out what went wrong. Then, build a better plan for the next attempt.
>
> _____
>
> _____
>
> _____
>
> _____
>
> _____
>
> _____

After the Raleigh location showed success, I decided to enter the Charleston market again. We again called on a few of our larger national customers and were able to land projects down there right away. We used the same process, commuting from Rock Hill to Charleston, doing the work, then traveling back in the evening.

It was like this for months. During some of the really heavy workloads, the guys would stay a night or two in a hotel to have plenty of time for the work. This also opened up the Myrtle Beach market for us, as it was managed alongside Charleston by several homebuilders.

Now my new problem was that I needed to be present at Rock Hill, Raleigh, Myrtle Beach, and Charleston each week. It was becoming very apparent that I was going to live on the road. Our Raleigh work was picking up, and much to our surprise, the larger customers started asking if we could travel even farther to the locations that their current vendors did not want to go to.

I immediately said yes, so now we were working in Wilmington and New Bern, North Carolina, which were five hours from our office. None of our competitors wanted to work there due to the location and travel time. The customers asked how much it would cost for us to provide service to these communities. We doubled the price of the close-proximity communities, and they agreed.

Now I really found myself in a conundrum. I had teen girls and a wife at home, and I was servicing a 763-mile area, visiting each of these locations every week. It took an entire week on the road to meet with everyone. By 2022, we were servicing the Charlotte metro area; Greenville, Charleston, and Myrtle Beach in South Carolina; Wilmington, New Bern, Raleigh, and Winston-Salem in North Carolina; and everywhere in between. This growth was fun and exciting, but being away from home this much was obviously not going to be sustainable. It was already beginning to show signs of wearing thin at home.

· · · · ·

My friend Mike (the landscaping guy I'd built a relationship with and played soccer against) had just expanded his landscaping business into a few locations, so I talked with him about my travel dilemma. He had the solution for me.

He introduced me to a guy named Jeff who owned a number of small, private turboprop airplanes. Mike suggested chartering a turboprop plane to travel between the different cities. I thought he was crazy, never imagining this in my wildest dreams, but it really made sense. I got my leadership team together, and we flew from city to city, meeting with our management team and customers.

Early in the morning in Charlotte, we would load up in a King Air turboprop airplane that seated six and touch down in Charleston within forty-five minutes. There would be a rental car waiting for us on the tarmac about forty feet from where our plane would come to a stop. We drove to meet with the selected crew and customer for a bit, then drove back to the airport for a quick twenty-minute flight to Myrtle Beach, where another rental car would be sitting on the tarmac waiting for us. We would again meet with the local team and customers. Then back to the airport for a quick thirty-minute flight to New Bern for meetings and lunch, followed by a flight to Raleigh for more meetings, and finally back to Charlotte. I was able to travel to every one of those cities, meet with our teams there, and still have dinner with my family that evening.

Shockingly, the cost of the flight wasn't much more than if we had rented hotel rooms and gas for the crew for the week. It was incredible!

I think the coolest thing we ever did was when one of the customers wanted a price quote on a new community that was way out of our path. The pilot asked us the address, and he dropped down to under one thousand feet and circled the property several times so we could get a good feel for the site conditions. We were able to give pricing for the community from the air!

There were a few people who asked why we didn't fly on commercial airlines. Well, the large airports were few and far between, and it took hours for security, boarding, deplaning, and finding ground transportation. Then there were still hours of driving to reach the remote locations. With the small turboprops, we had the advantage of finding small landing strips that were never more than a fifteen-minute drive to the site, and there was no security and no lines. Just strap in and wheels up! That is what enabled us to hit all the locations in one day.

On several occasions, the homebuilders would ask us to give them a price for the work in a new coastal community that they were ready to start. While we were commuting between locations, I would give the pilot the location of the new community, and he would drop down and circle the property as many times as needed so we could see the whole property to price it. This charter flight enabled me to do all this traveling and be home to spend time with my family—not to mention it was so much fun!

A few times, people would ask, "How did you get here so fast? Weren't you just in Charleston this morning?"

"Man, we were *flying*!" I'd reply.

They usually assumed I meant we were driving fast, but I never corrected them.

· · · · ·

In life, you have to either give up time or money. I had the choice to save money and drive to these locations, and it would have been mostly fun, but my family and relationships would have suffered. I chose time over money—and it paid off. You always have to give something up to grow. It might be money. It might be time. It might be ego. It might be a bad habit. Growth will always have a cost. Always be on the lookout for a better way. Flying using a turboprop airplane did not seem logical at first, but it enabled us to open all these other locations in a two-year time span!

Growth will always have a cost. Always be on the lookout for a better way.

29

SMALL TOWNS, BIG WINS
The Power of Niche Markets

The big question was where to expand after we started getting traction in Raleigh and Charleston. Florida and Georgia were booming markets, but they were also super crowded with competitors. We would have to compete on price, which is a race to the bottom. As we looked at the major cities, we realized that most of the cities were paying a lower price than we were currently getting. To enter these cities, we would have to enter the market with steep discounts just to get traction.

The more we studied the situation, the more we kept coming back to D.R. Horton. They were one of our newer customers, as we had only been working for them for a couple of years in Charlotte. They are the biggest homebuilder in America and are a Fortune

500 company, which means they are one of the five hundred biggest companies in America by revenue.

As I looked over our possibilities, I noticed that D.R. Horton was expanding to build homes in areas and into small towns where there was next to no home-building competition. They would either set up shop there or buy a small local builder and convert them to the D.R. Horton model.

As I made a few calls, I realized there were also no subcontractors that were ready for the large home-builder systems. This made it easy to sell our services to them because we were a plug-and-play subcontractor. D.R. Horton had proprietary software, including their purchase order system, that required the sub-contractors to have a uniquely trained office staff. The national homebuilders like D.R. Horton also needed large insurance policies for liability and workers comp, which none of the local trades seemed to have.

I realized it would be easy to get into these new markets with a higher-than-normal price. It was attractive for D.R. Horton to have a subcontractor that knew their systems and was insurance com-pliant. They could just focus on their growth instead of training new companies in every new town they entered. We were able to charge sometimes up to three times our normal price for the same work because we were in these small markets where there was zero competition.

This became very profitable for us, although it did cause a lot of windshield time—which is what we call it when the guys have to drive in rural areas and sit behind the windshield of the truck instead of billing—but we more than made up for it in our pricing. This also made us the first call for an expansion when D.R. Horton had trouble with subcontractors, because they realized we were willing to go to new places with them.

Your customers will almost always let you know of problems they are struggling to solve if you take the time to talk with them. So many people simply do their task and then race to the next task. But it is almost always worth it to slow down and make it a practice to ask, "Are there any other areas that I can help with?" and "Is there any problem or challenge I can help you solve?"

> *Your customers will almost always let you know of problems they are struggling to solve if you take the time to talk with them.*

They will almost always have more, and this is your chance to help solve it. If you show that you can solve their problems, you will be the first person they call when a problem arises, which means you have the first shot at earning their business. Do not immediately turn down work simply because it is unattractive. See if there is a price point that can make it worth doing.

NO COLLEGE, NO PROBLEM

Of course, some of these opportunities will be worthwhile, and some won't be. For example, one of our national customers reached out to see if we would have any interest in providing service for them in Virginia. We decided not to pursue this because we had our sights on Tennessee, Florida, and Georgia.

We had a similar situation in our next expansion target, Nashville, Tennessee. We had several connections in the area, and the city was experiencing rapid growth. After investigating multiple times, we concluded that the terrain posed significant challenges—rocky and difficult to work with—especially compared to the softer, sandier conditions along the coast. In coastal areas, our crews could install more fences per hour, with far less wear and tear on the equipment. While Nashville's construction market was thriving, we recognized that other locations offered better profitability due to the more favorable working conditions.

· · · · ·

Word travels fast when you are helping people solve problems. Unfortunately, in this situation, the Tennessee market was a less profitable opportunity for us, so we selected different locations, but having the option was nice. Resources are not infinite, so you need to choose your opportunities wisely.

✍ **ACTION:** Take time to plan your expansion. Growth is not always the right answer.

_____

_____

_____

_____

_____

_____

30

AN UNEXPECTED OFFER

Negotiation, Determination, and Silence

It was November 2021, and we had just started to focus on expanding into Georgia and Florida, when I arrived at the office to one of my staff members handing me the business card of a recent visitor. This happened quite often. It seemed that people would stop by daily to visit or meet.

On this occasion, I called the number on the card, and he told me the nature of his visit: He wanted to buy my business! He asked for a meeting, and I reluctantly agreed. He said he had driven through the night to meet me.

He began to state his case. He had sold a portion of his company to a private equity firm. That private equity firm had also bought a stake in six other environmental companies in Tennessee, Texas, and South Carolina, with the intention of consolidating them into one large environmental company. My business was the next link in the chain because we had the lion's share of the work in North and South Carolina, and apparently, we had been competing with his heavily funded company with deep pockets for a while now.

This man was there to meet with me as a representative partially for his company and partially for the private equity firm—a joint venture. They had purchased six or seven of the companies around me. I was familiar with several of them, but I didn't notice they were actively trying to take market share, because we were rapidly gaining our own market share. He went on to say that, for them, we were the key to the Carolinas.

After he finished his presentation, I told him I had no interest in selling my company. "I know you have plenty of money and you are much bigger than us," I said. "I am sure you will do great and make it hard on us, but I feel good about what we are doing."

This next exchange took me completely by surprise. He looked down at the floor, and then he said, "Do you know the story of Gideon in the Bible?" I did know the story but not very well. In the story, Gideon led a small army of 300 men against an enemy army of 135,000 men—and claimed victory.

He then went on to say, "Guys like you may have a small army, but you can't be beat. Just think about my offer. It could free you up to do new things in this season of your life."

I didn't know what to say at that point. I thanked him for his time.

> ✏ **ACTION:** Always take meetings. There is always something to learn. At the very least, I left that meeting with the knowledge that my competitors saw us as unbeatable! How cool is that?
>
> _____
>
> _____
>
> _____
>
> _____
>
> _____
>
> _____

Roughly once every couple of weeks, the interested buyer would reach out "to see how I was doing." I would reply that we were fine. Then, just before Christmas, he asked if he could send a letter of intent to buy my company with a proposed price. I said sure but that I didn't think we could come to any kind of agreement.

He said, "You might want to consider the freedom that it could bring to have some cash and be able to pursue other things you may be interested in."

He sent over a letter of intent (LOI) just after Christmas.

Tracy and I must have read that letter fifty times over the next week. We would go on daily walks and discuss what it would be like to sell, what we would need financially to make it work, what we would do after the acquisition—because we both believe in hard work. We ended up making a counteroffer, which resulted in him being offended.

"I have never paid any company a number like that," he said.

The talks immediately ended. He was hot. I was annoyed.

I pulled my senior leadership team into our meeting room to tell them about the encounter and the purpose of it. I wanted to know if the team would like the idea of being part of a bigger company with opportunities to move up higher. It was too big of a deal to keep it to myself. Plus, if I were in their shoes, I would have wanted to know that things were possibly about to change.

The response was a mix of "we want you to do what is best for you," and "we didn't come because we love erosion control; we came because we believed in you." This did not make the decision-making process easier, but it did tell me where they stood.

📝 **ACTION:** Be open with your inner circle. Don't give every detail, and don't inform every person, but give information to the leadership team. Give them time to process what is going on. Also, a buyer is going to want to meet people, and your integrity will be in danger if you try to sneak around. You will be surprised by what you hear from your team. Treat others the way you want to be treated. They will appreciate being in the inner circle and being trusted.

_____

_____

_____

_____

_____

_____

NO COLLEGE, NO PROBLEM

• • • • •

I began a whiteboard session with our leadership team to plan out our new and improved strategy to continue with our growth plan. Everyone was fired up as we met almost daily to refine and execute the plans. As the days passed, we continued to grow and gain momentum.

About a month later, a man named Jordan from the private equity firm called me. He went on to say that he would like to pick the negotiations back up.

But in the time since the previous guy had flown off the handle, my team and I had come up with awesome plans to really pour gas on our business to grow even faster. Knowing that the behemoth company was out there lurking only fired our team up more. We were ready to get after it!

I told Jordan that I didn't see how it would work, that we were too far apart to try to piece it back together, and I thanked him for his time. Over the next couple of weeks, he reached out to me several times, and on his last time reaching out, he finally asked, "Well, what do you want for the company?"

I told him the number I wanted. He went quiet. We sat in complete silence. I was pretty annoyed, so I didn't care.

I later discovered that silence is a great negotiation tactic. I would love to claim that was my plan, but I truly was just annoyed.

Jordan's response finally came after what felt like a couple of minutes: "Okay."

I asked him what their plan would be for me, and he said, "You won't even notice the company sold except when you look at your bank account. We want you to run it the way you always have. Nothing will change."

That sounded perfect.

Of course, I learned later that "nothing will change" in private equity language is easily translated to "everything will change."

· · · · ·

Patience has been one of my hardest lessons, and I'm still working on it. I like to move fast and be decisive. But over the years, I had to learn to take difficult calls and slow down to truly listen.

---

*I had to learn to take difficult calls
and slow down to truly listen.*

That wasn't how I started the business—if I had listened to some people then, I would've never started at all. But as we enter new seasons in life and business, growth requires adapting—and that almost always means listening more.

FROM HARD WORK TO HARD EARNED

The Closing Chapter

I couldn't believe we had just made a deal, but I was somehow able to keep quiet. Jordan said he would be back in touch. I would like to claim that this was my plan all along—to hold out for more money—but it wasn't.

When the earlier negotiations fell apart, we started making plans. We had made ourselves completely ready for a fierce all-out competition. Now I had to change gears back into the mindset of a potential sale of the company.

My finance team and I spent the next couple of months sorting through transactions for the previous few years' accounting books. We had to label whether each transaction was qualified to be an add-back, which would then be added to the bottom line. There was also a barrage of questions and data coming from the accountant of the private equity firm during our due diligence period.

We must have sat at that conference table for two hundred hours over the next couple of months. It was tough but well worth it. In my final year, we were on a run rate in excess of $18 million in revenue with more than one hundred employees in six cities.

After eight arduous months of due diligence, closing day finally came. My energy and anxiety were off the charts. Was this really going to happen? Was I really selling my twenty-year project? Would I really get paid that much? I just could not wrap my head around it.

The private equity firm was borrowing money to buy my company, and we had to wait on their bank for the necessary paperwork. It was the most anticlimactic ending ever.

We received an email around 4:00 p.m. that it had closed and that the money should be in my account by the next day. It was nothing like you see in the movies. The attorneys were on the phone with each other, but my CFO and I just sat in silence at my conference table.

In the end, there was no phone call, no lawyers, no signing actual papers, no handshake—just an email that it was complete.

• • • • •

Some of the biggest events in life don't come with trumpets and sirens. I had expected some big production, but it ended with a simple email. For the private equity firm and the lawyers, it was just another day's work and another deal, similar to how I viewed the days when I took our business into a new city. But for me, it was the first time in my life since childhood that I was completely debt-free! This was an ending of sorts for me—and a new beginning.

Some of the biggest events in life don't come with trumpets and sirens.

The next day, I brought my leadership team together and told them that it had closed and that I was not the owner anymore. I had been open with them from the very beginning about what was going on, from the first time I was approached. I did not share every detail, but I believe we should treat others the way we want to be treated, and I would have wanted to know.

I told them that I was now an employee, the same as them. Everyone was quiet except for small chatter. For hours, it felt like a funeral. Everyone was happy that I had achieved my dream of being debt-free, but it was a weird feeling. The energy just immediately left the group.

• • • • •

It's important to take the time to build a team that cares. The sale hit everyone hard because our leadership team was so united, but it was just the end of one era and the beginning of another. It wasn't long before everyone was back at it and marching forward.

Honestly, the toughest part of the whole acquisition was feeling like I lost the team I built. This was a tough reality, and it took me several weeks to get used to it. I was used to talking to my leadership team every single day, mostly about work, but also we caught up about family and life.

When you sell your company, there will be changes. Prepare for them. The day after the sale, you are not the owner anymore. I stayed on for roughly a month after the sale, but as the days passed, it became clear that it was not a good fit. So I reached out to my new supervisor and made him aware that I was leaving. After all, it was their company now, and I had a new chapter to start!

✎ **ACTION:** If you are considering a sale of your business, we can help you walk through this. Find out more at CoreBusinessEssentials .com.

_____

_____

_____

_____

_____

_____

32

HALFTIME

The Journey Beyond the Deal

As I think back on my business venture, I realize it was one wild ride. The excitement of my big payoff is not what I reflect on the most—though it did make it possible to retire at age forty-seven. Rather, I think back on the amazing twenty-year journey that built and shaped me.

I could never have learned what I did anywhere else. There are only a handful of organizations that encourage the team to learn and grow. We were able to build a company where people were free to think, and if anyone on the team had an idea, we would give them room to run with the idea. We would collaborate on almost every single project.

During those twenty years, I got to hire people and watch them grow and mature. I watched them buy their first houses, get married, and have babies. I learned as much from them as they did from me.

I learned as much from them as they did from me.

It has been two years now since the acquisition. I do sometimes wonder where we could have taken the company if I was still at the helm.

Whether to sell your business or not is a tough decision. We had built an unstoppable team, and we had fun doing it! Here are things to consider about selling your business that are not hyped on Instagram and YouTube, such as:

1. Your team will no longer be yours—they'll focus on pleasing the new owner.
2. The momentum you worked hard to build will transfer with the company in exchange for your payout. The momentum goes with the company.
3. The customers and vendors will be happy for you, but their new job is to maintain their new relationship.
4. You'll be seen differently—no longer a peer in the workforce, but part of the privileged "1 percent." Trust me, it will be different.

5. Be prepared for your company to shift from passionate and productive to one driven by corporate processes and systems.

I began to wonder if these feelings I was experiencing were only mine. I began to search out people who shared my circumstances. What I experienced, even down to the day of closing, is actually more typical than what I expected to find. Some people even fall into depression with the loss of identity.

As for me, the original guy who came to negotiate with me was right. Selling has enabled me to do things that I never dreamed of! We bought a catamaran and sailed it from Maryland to the Exumas. We spent a week at a time exploring the islands of the Exumas, sailing around them and anchoring out when we were ready for a rest. It was an experience like no other—just my family and the open sea with crystal-clear waters.

I also took some time to read the book *Halftime: Moving from Success to Significance* by Bob Buford. I won't spoil it, but I highly recommend it. It astounded me that my life seemed to be following what he laid out in his book. I was beginning the second half of my life, which meant it was time to stop trying to achieve significance in the workplace and begin to help others on the journey of where I was twenty years ago.

So many people try to recreate their twenties and thirties in their forties and fifties, but it will never be fulfilling. Who we are in our forties is a new creature. It is time to write a new chapter and stop chasing the old wins of our early working careers. *Halftime* is an amazing book that really helped lead me after the acquisition.

I have discovered since the sale of my company and after sailing on and off for a year that I love business. I love the wins, the struggles, the excitement, the working together to solve problems.

And just think . . . none of this would have been possible if it hadn't been for the excellent advice of my high school guidance counselors and teachers who said, "You have to go to college unless you want to dig ditches for a living!"

If they hadn't prepared me for a life of digging ditches, I would have missed out on this journey, and I would have been stuck with college debt and a J-O-B!

AFTERWORD
TURNING EXPERIENCE
INTO IMPACT
Coaching for Change

I have now found myself guiding and mentoring small-business leaders who want to grow and see what they can achieve, and Tracy has developed content specifically for the spouses of entrepreneurs, helping them navigate these unique challenges.

We have been able to help so many leaders avoid or conquer some of the obstacles that had me stuck early on. It has been amazing to use our story to help others and to see their reaction when they finally realize there *is* a way to get out of whatever situation they're stuck in. If I had known to get a coach or mentor when I crossed the $1 million mark, who knows what could have been possible?

If you are on this business journey, if you're considering or in the process of selling your business, or if you simply want to dream again, you're not alone. We're here to help! Just shoot us a message, and we'll guide you every step of the way.

www.CoreBusinessEssentials.com

APPENDIX A

BOOKS THAT HELPED SHAPE ME

- *Failing Forward* by John C. Maxwell
- *Good to Great* by Jim Collins
- *Halftime* by Bob Buford
- *Rhinoceros Success* by Scott Alexander
- *Rich Dad Poor Dad* by Robert T. Kiyosaki
- *Sometimes You Win, Sometimes You Learn* by John C. Maxwell
- *The 21 Irrefutable Laws of Leadership* by John C. Maxwell
- *The E-Myth Revisited* by Michael E. Gerber
- *The Go-Getter* by Peter B. Kyne
- *The Legend of the Monk and the Merchant* by Terry Felber
- *The Millionaire Next Door* by Thomas J. Stanley, PhD and William D. Danko, PhD
- *Thou Shall Prosper* by Rabbi Daniel Lapin
- *Who Moved My Cheese?* by Spencer Johnson, MD

APPENDIX B

MY REVENUE TIMELINE

2003: $16K

2004: $380K

2005: $520K

2006: $994K

2007: $760K

2008: $330K

2009: $200K

2010: $375K

2011: $550K

2012: $750K

2013: $1.1M

2014: $2.3M

2015: $3.4M

2016: $5.4M

2017: $7.2M

2018: $8.8M

2019: $8M

2020: $12M

2021: $15M

2022: $18M

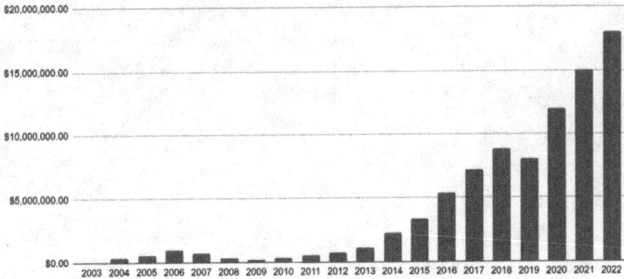

ACKNOWLEDGMENTS

Every person I have ever encountered—friends, family, and even brief acquaintances—has played at least some role in shaping my journey. Each interaction, no matter how small, has contributed to the successes, challenges, and lessons that have been woven into this book. To everyone who has crossed my path, I am deeply grateful. Your influence, whether direct or indirect, is part of the story recorded here.

Special thanks to Jessica Sly, Rachel Miller, Phil Lanier, and Tracy Lanier for final editing and helping bring this book to life.

ABOUT THE AUTHOR

Phillip Lanier is an entrepreneur, business coach, and author dedicated to helping CEOs reclaim their personal time, build stronger connections with their teams, and grow successful companies with integrity. As the founder of Business Essentials and GrowthGears, Phillip teaches business leaders how to scale with purpose while balancing the demands of leadership and a fulfilling personal life. His coaching has empowered countless individuals to lead with vision and enjoy the journey with their teams. When he is not coaching or writing, Phillip enjoys wake-surfing, Spikeball, and anything outdoors, driven by his passion for making a lasting impact in the lives of others.

NOTES

1. Bailee Hill, "Mike Rowe Sounds Alarm over 'Scary' Trade Worker Shortage: US on 'Verge of Not Being Able to Make Stuff,'" FOX Business, June 21, 2024, https://www.foxbusiness.com/media/mike-rowe -sounds-alarm-scary-trade-worker-shortage-us-verge -not-being-able-make-stuff.

2. Andrew Dorn, "Labor Crisis: Why Is There a Shortage of Plumbers and Electricians?," The Hill, April 9, 2024, https://thehill.com/changing-america /enrichment/education/4583268-labor-crisis-why-is -there-a-shortage-of-plumbers-and-electricians/.

3. Melanie Hanson, "Average Cost of College & Tuition," Education Data Initiative, March 8, 2025, https://educationdata.org/average-cost-of-college.

4. Melanie Hanson, "Student Loan Debt by Income Level," Education Data Initiative, October 12, 2024, https:// educationdata.org/student-loan-debt-by-income-level.

5. "Bachelor Degree Salary: Hourly Rate May 2025 USA," ZipRecruiter, accessed June 16, 2025, https://www .ziprecruiter.com/Salaries/Bachelor-Degree-Salary.

6. "Skilled Trade Salary in South Carolina," Zip Recruiter, accessed April 5, 2025, https://www.ziprecruiter.com /Salaries/Skilled-Trade-Salary--in-South-Carolina.
7. Learn more about Dave Ramsey's teaching and offerings at www.ramseysolutions.com.